For my mom
NANCY K. NICHOLAS
who put yarn, needles,
fibers, fabrics,
and color
into my
life

contents

The Knitting Palette

27 stunning colour inspired designs

KRISTIN NICHOLAS

David and Charles

A DAVID & CHARLES BOOK

© 2007 by Storey Publishing

David & Charles is an F+W Publications Inc. company

4700 East Galbraith Road

Cincinnati, OH 45236

First published in the UK in 2008

Originally published in the United States of America by Storey Publishing 210 MASS
MoCA Way, North Adams, MA 01247.

For Storey Publishing:

Edited by Gwen Steege and Lori Gayle

Art direction, cover, and text design by Cynthia N. McFarland

Text production by Jennifer Jepson Smith

Photography by Kevin Kennefick

Illustrations by Kristin Nicholas

Indexed by Mary McClintock

A catalogue record for this book is available from the British Library.

ISBN-13: 978-0-7153-2918-4 paperback
ISBN-10: 0-7153-2918-9 paperback

Printed in China by Dai Nippon Printing
for David & Charles
Brunel House   Newton Abbot   Devon

Visit our website at www.davidandcharles.co.uk

David & Charles books are available from all good bookshops; alternatively you can
contact our Orderline on 0870 9908222 or write to us at FREEPOST EX2 110, D&C
Direct, Newton Abbot, TQ12 4ZZ (no stamp required UK only); US customers call
800-289-0963 and Canadian customers call 800-840-5220.

MARVELOUS MITTENS & GLOVES   104

STUNNING SWEATERS   140

BACK TO THE BASICS   190

INDEX   207

WORKING
WITH
COLOR

I love color! As a knitter, you are probably obsessed by color, too. A beautiful color in just the right texture or fiber can make you spend 10 times as much as you had planned on yarn for a project. A color can make you feel good about yourself, your knitting techniques shine, and your hours knitting just plain joyous and happy. You probably know which colors are your favorites, which look the best on you, and which ones you're just plain terrified of. What I hope to help you learn on the pages of this book is how to combine colors in a creative way to make a piece of knitwear that is more a piece of color art than anything else. You'll learn my way of working with color, which is definitely not the only way. Once you understand how I combine and work with colors, however, I hope you'll develop your unique color sense and make it your signature style.

Kristin Nicholas

knitting and color

Knitting with color can be as simple as making stripes — thin ones, fat ones, even ones and uneven ones. It can be making a solid sweater and then tipping the ribbed edges with just a row of a contrast color. Adding simple embroidery techniques on a solid-colored knit can make a project playful and memorable. Or go completely over the top and mix all kinds of Fair Isle patterns together, decorate them with embroidery, and turn them into a riot of color exploration.

You can spend your entire life learning about how colors work together. I know I have. When you are working with color, experimentation is key. As you experiment, observe, and play, you'll develop your own innate color sense. Best of all, you can have fun, dive in, and not be afraid. You can always rip it out.

IT'S A PERSONAL THING

I am always amazed by the number of knitters who knit the colors just as shown on a pattern leaflet or in a book. Sometimes I observe conversations in yarn stores, and I especially get a kick out of women talking to their men or children while picking out a sweater to knit for them. The intended recipient puts the kibosh on a sweater because he doesn't understand that it can be knit in a color different from that shown in the photo. Although this may seem to be an extreme example, it happens frequently. I think it's because people who don't knit, don't understand the planning and conceptual stage of any design.

If you're timid about color, by all means, knit the projects in this book in the same colors that I've shown. But I hope that after reading these few pages, you'll be brave enough to try picking out a colorway of your own.

GILDING THE LILY

Adding embroidery on knits is a great way to add interest and fun to a plain knitted fabric. It's relatively simple to do, with only a few simple guidelines to follow. In a matter of a few short minutes, you can completely alter the feel of a finished garment.

The first thing is to conquer your misgivings. In this book, I've used only six easy embroidery stitches that work well for decorating knitted fabric. As with any new technique, it's best to practice on a swatch to gain confidence to master the technique.

seeing is believing — and learning

The easiest way to learn about color is to begin observing life around you. Here's a fun color exercise: Open up your pantry shelves and start pulling packages out. Pasta boxes, anchovy and tuna cans, cracker boxes, juice boxes — all matters of packaging. Look at them — really look at them. Decide what you are most attracted to and then think about what makes you like it? Is it the base color? Is it the type? Is it how the colors are combined? Observe and study everything you come in contact with for an entire day, keeping a little notebook or perhaps taking digital pictures. You'll soon start to notice how graphic designers use color to make you want to pick up a product and actually buy it. How many times have you purchased a bar of soap or a bottle of wine expressly because you liked the label? Probably quite a few. And lots of times, it's because you're attracted to the colors on the label and how they are used together.

You can do the same exercise while flipping through pages of a magazine. It's fun and, by the time you're done, you'll have learned something about how others work with color as well as which colors you are attracted to. I am a perennial ripper — I tear ideas from magazines and catalogs all the time. I stack them up and then take another look at them after a few months. Sometimes I can't remember what I liked about the page and it gets filed in the trash. But from some of these ideas, I recharge my design batteries and come up with my own new color combinations and knit patterns.

Visiting a local museum or gallery or taking art books out of your local library can help you learn how artists work with color. Art is so much about color and how colors relate to each other to create a pleasing composition. By looking at what appears on canvas, you can further develop your comfort level with color. I always stop at the museum gift shop and pick up a few pretty postcards to display on my studio walls. They are a good tool to help subliminal absorption of how someone else successfully and beautifully uses color. (See samples, page 11.)

Mother Nature can be the best teacher of all. Around you in the natural world, the earth is full of beautiful colors. Those colors are naturally combined with other shades to make interesting and exciting combinations. A quick walk on a hiking trail or a stroll through your garden or a public park can fill you with color combination ideas for years to come. Take along a digital camera to document the ideas, and you'll have a record to refer to when you begin designing.

Use Mother Nature's color combinations to inspire your choice of palette for your next knitting project.

the design process

When I'm designing a color combination for a project, I start out by gathering the balls of yarn I think I may want to use for a base color. I hold them together and look at them and decide if they are what I want for the project I have in my head. I take them outside to see how they work together in natural light. Then I begin adding other colors to see how they would enhance the base colors I've chosen. It's a very visual process and one that is hard to explain. But it is how I begin every project.

SWATCHING

Next, I take the yarn I think I want to make the project from, and I cast on with the base color. I knit a swatch out of the pattern and the colors I have chosen. Usually by the third or fourth row, I can tell if the color combination is going to work out. If I like it and it is visually pleasing, I keep going. If not, I cast off, setting it aside to remind myself not to use that combination again. I keep all my swatches and often refer back to them. They are wonderful visual diaries of how colors work together, why certain combinations are successful, and certain ones not. Someday I'm going to sew them all together and make a giant blanket for our bed.

I've tried to design projects on my computer in Adobe Illustrator (a very sophisticated computer drawing tool). Computers are great and I use them in my work daily, but when it comes to designing knitwear, I've found there's nothing better than an old-fashioned swatch. The computer screen lacks the depth and physical texture of yarn and stitches. There is just nothing more important to me in my daily design work than the handknit swatch.

CRAFTING COLOR COMBOS. The same gold background yarn was used to knit all five of these swatches. Note how the second, contrasting color changes the feeling of the finished fabric.

INCORPORATING ARTIST TOOLS

Every art-supply store sells color wheels. Developed by Sir Isaac Newton in 1666, the color wheel is made up of 12 slices. Colors that are opposite each other on the wheel are complementary colors. For me, these combinations of colors are the most exciting to play with. Orange and turquoise shades pop and vibrate against each other to stimulate my mind — similar to visiting the desert of the Southwest. Green and red, like the combination of colors of a coleus leaf, jump about. Yellow and violet, like the colors on the cheerful faces of pansies, make me smile.

If you find complementary color combinations too garish, you can pick shades that are close together on the wheel, such as purple, red, and orange. You'll get a more tonal-looking knit fabric that creates a more soothing feeling, similar to an amazing sunset.

COLOR WHEELS AS TOOLS. Use a color wheel to discover complementary color combinations (those directly opposite one another, such as yellow and purple or red and green) that can make your project come alive.

UNDERSTANDING VALUE

When I design knitwear, I like my motifs to stand out from one another, so that the knitted design is clearly delineated. One way is to choose complementary colors as I just described, but the other is to choose shades that differ in value (darkness and lightness) from each other.

The six swatches shown here use the same knitted design, but are worked in combinations with varying differences in color value. Notice how each one gives a totally different feeling from the others.

EVERYTHING IS NOT EITHER BLACK OR WHITE

Perhaps you've noticed by now that I haven't mentioned black or white. This has become one of my trademarks — I don't use either of these colors at all. White is boring to me, and I must admit that some of these prejudices against black and white come from working for a yarn company. Blacks and whites are always the best-selling colors in any yarn. I wanted to promote color, so I always designed with colors knowing that there would be no problem selling black and white. As the years have progressed and I no longer worry about sales of yarn colors, I still don't design with black or white — to me they aren't interesting and they just don't add zing to a garment. It is more difficult to design with colors only, but once you begin to, you too will be addicted.

STUDIES IN COMPLEMENTS AND VALUES. Each of these swatch pairings demonstrates a color principle: (top left) The complementary hues of the diamonds on the blue background are the same, but their values are very different; (bottom left) the swatch below illustrates a very high-contrast color combination, while the yarns at the top are in low contrast to one another; (directly above) using the same colors but reversing them in the design creates entirely different effects.

a personal note

I HAVE SPENT my entire life learning about, experimenting with, and being seduced by color. We moved to a new house when I was eight years old. I remember the minty-green walls of the kitchen, the old color-splotched linoleum floors, and the huge, white, cast-iron sink. In fact, the former owners had painted most of the house with green-colored walls — what we referred to as "hospital green" — a shade that to this day, I am not fond of. My mom soon began to turn that new house into *our* family's home, pouring over decorating magazines, wallpaper books, and paint chips. She agonized over her decisions, with my dad in full support, adding his two cents as to whether he liked the colors she chose or not.

As she decorated, a color theme became evident to my young eyes: my mom loved golds, oranges, browns, and reds — warm shades. She combined all kinds of fabrics and tones to make a warm and inviting home for my sisters, my dad, me, and our friends. To this day, I can remember asking her about her choices. I noticed that there wasn't an inch of blue anywhere in her décor. Her response was that her mom had loved blue, and her entire childhood home was blue. She had had enough blue in her life. She was making her own statement with her home — that she was different from her mom.

Color, no matter how trivial some may think it, is paramount to my existence. I live, breathe, and eat color. I can't get enough of it. As an adult, I've forged through color fashions and fantasies while working as a colorist and marketing director of a yarn company. I've read color forecast after color forecast, always curious to see what the "color experts" see as the next big trend. I know how color can make a person feel: joyous, sad, pensive, or quiet. I like to know what the next hot color is, what is selling the best, but now I take in the forecasting information and work with the "new" colors to suit my own tastes and needs.

Sensational
SCARVES
&
ONE AFGHAN

polka dot
scarf

Scarves are perfect first projects for beginners, and this one with different kinds of polka dot trims will please young and old. Because I find scarves very tedious to knit lengthwise, I came up with the idea for knitting the scarf sideways on circular needles, so that the scarf is finished quickly. I added a bit of interest to this very plain garter stitch scarf by decorating it with different kinds of polka dots. On the bright pink scarf (version 1), they are handmade pompoms; on the green-gold scarf (version 2), the polka dots are embroidered; and on the periwinkle scarf (version 3) the dots are knitted bobbles. Each one has pompoms along the bottom edge to give a bouncy, fun feel to this easy scarf. Garter stitch is a great choice because not only is it reversible, but the fabric lies nice and flat.

Plan of action: The scarf is knitted back and forth on circular needles, starting from the long edge. This requires many stitches but few rows. The different versions allow you to choose among arrangements of pompoms, spider-web embroidery, and/or bobbles for decoration.

stitches

> **GARTER STITCH**
> Knit all stitches every row.

SIZES AND FINISHED MEASUREMENTS

Child, 42½" × 6" (108 cm × 15 cm)
Adult, 64" × 10" (162.5 cm × 25.5 cm)
Models shown are adult size.

GAUGE

16 stitches and 35 rows = 4" (10 cm) in Garter Stitch.

NEEDLES

US 9 (5.5 mm) circular needle 29" (75 cm) long *or size you need to obtain the correct gauge*

NOTIONS

Tapestry needle
Pompom maker (optional) or scrap cardboard

YARN

Nashua Handknits Julia, 50% wool/ 25% mohair/25% alpaca, 93 yd (85 m)/ 1¾ oz (50 g). Yarn band gauge: 5 stitches and 6 rows = 1" (2.5 cm) in Stockinette Stitch on US 7 (4.5 mm) needles.

Version 1:
MC= 5084 Zinnia Pink, 4 skeins for Child; 6 skeins for Adult

CC = 5185 Spring Green, 2 skeins for both sizes

Version 2:
MC= 3691 Ladies Mantle, 4 skeins for Child; 6 skeins for Adult

CC = 8118 Espresso, 1 skein for both sizes

Version 3:
MC = 5178 Lupine, 4 skeins for Child; 6 skeins for Adult

CA = 2250 French Pumpkin, 1 skein for both sizes

CB = 2163 Golden Honey, 1 skein for both sizes

CC = 5185 Spring Green, 1 skein for both sizes

CD = 2083 Magenta, 1 skein for both sizes

CE = 8141 Pretty Pink, 1 skein for both sizes

CAST-ON TIPS

Casting on loosely for the scarves that are knit vertically is very important, otherwise one side of the scarf may be longer than the other. To make sure your cast-on stitches stay loose, try these tricks:

▸ For the cast on, use needles two sizes larger than those called for in the pattern, then change to the recommended size for the first row.

▸ Place two needles side by side and cast on over both of them, then remove one of the needles as you work the first row.

▸ Concentrate very hard to make a loose cast on.

Note You can use these same techniques if you have problems with your cast-off being too tight.

KNITTING THE SCARF	CHILD	ADULT
Set Up With MC and taking care to make your cast on neither too loose nor too tight (see above), cast on	170 sts	255 sts
Next Rows Work in Garter Stitch for	6" (15 cm)	10" (25.5 cm)
Bind off all stitches.		

FINISHING

Weave in ends.

VERSION 1

Using CC make 11 pompoms for the Child's scarf and 17 pompoms for the Adult's scarf. (For how to make pompoms, see page 199.) Using MC, attach 3 pompoms on each end of the Child's scarf and 5 pompoms on the end of the Adult's scarf (see facing page). Then attach remaining pompoms randomly over the main fabric of the scarf.

VERSION 2

Pompoms. Using CC, make 6 pompoms for the Child's scarf and 10 pompoms for the Adult's scarf. Using MC, attach the pompoms to the short ends of the scarf, with 3 pompoms on each end of the Child's scarf and 5 pompoms on the end of the Adult's scarf.

Embroidery. Using CC, embroider 15 to 18 randomly placed spider web stitch motifs (see page 198), each about ¾" (2 cm) in diameter.

Bobbles. With each of the 5 contrast colors, make 4 bobbles for the Child's scarf (a total of 20 bobbles) and 6 bobbles for the Adult's scarf (a total of 30 bobbles), according to the instructions below.

KNITTING THE BOBBLES

Set Up Cast on 1 stitch.

Row 1 (right side) Knit into the front, back, front, and back of same stitch to make 4 stitches from the single cast on stitch.

Rows 2 and 4 (wrong side) P4.

Row 3 K4.

Row 5 K4, pass second, third, and fourth stitches on needle over the first stitch to decrease back to 1 stitch.

Cut yarn, leaving a 5" (12.5 cm) tail, and fasten off last stitch.

With the purl side of the bobble facing out, tie the cast on and bind off tails together. Attach bobbles randomly placed on scarf as follows: Use a tapestry needle to pull both bobble tails through to the wrong side of the fabric, knot the ends, pull both tails back to the right side of the fabric, and weave the tails into the center of the bobble as stuffing to create a nice, rounded shape.

Pompoms. Using various combinations of the 5 contrast colors as shown, make 8 pompoms for the Child's scarf and 12 pompoms for the Adult's scarf. Using MC, sew 4 pompoms evenly spaced on each short end of the Child's scarf and 6 pompoms on each end of the Adult's scarf.

Attaching the bobble.

Attaching the pompom.

dotty striped scarf

Vertical stripes become the design focus on this easy-to-knit garter stitch scarf. Because it is worked sideways on circular needles, you don't need to work with more than one color at a time: Each band of color simply begins at the start of a new row. The polka dots that decorate each side of the teal blue stripes are French knots, stitched into the garter stitch "ditches" after the knitting is done. Although not truly reversible, if the embroidery is stitched neatly, the wrong side has its own kind of design (see page 22). Multicolored pompoms add a swingy feel to the bottom edges.

Plan of action: Circular needles provide the length needed for many stitches, although the scarf is knitted back and forth, not in the round. French knots and pompoms are added at the end.

stitches

GARTER STITCH
Knit all stitches every row.

FINISHED MEASUREMENTS
58" × 8½" (147.5 cm × 21.5 cm)

GAUGE
17½ stitches and 40 rows = 4" (10 cm) in Garter Stitch.

NEEDLES
US 8 (5 mm) circular needle 29" (75 cm) long *or size you need to obtain the correct gauge*

NOTIONS
Tapestry needle
Pompom maker (optional) or scrap cardboard

YARN
Nashua Handknits Julia, 50% wool/ 25% mohair/25% alpaca, 93 yd (85 m)/ 1¾ oz (50 g). Yarn band gauge: 5 stitches and 6 rows = 1" (2.5 cm) in Stockinette Stitch on US 7 (4.5 mm) needles.

CA = 8118 Espresso, 2 skeins

CB = 4936 Blue Thyme, 1 skein

CC = 2083 Magenta, 4 skeins

KNITTING THE SCARF

Set Up Using CA, cast on 255 stitches, taking care to make your cast on neither too loose nor too tight (see page 18).

Next Rows Knit 7 rows in Garter Stitch ending with a wrong side row, to complete 4 garter ridges, including the cast on row.

Next Rows Change to CB and knit 8 rows.

Next Rows Change to CA and knit 8 rows. Piece measures about 2½" (6.5 cm) from cast on.

Next Rows Change to CC and knit 34 rows. Piece measures about 6" (15 cm) from cast on.

Next Rows Change to CB and knit 8 rows.

Next Rows Change to CA and knit 7 rows, ending with a right side row.

Next Row (wrong side) Using CA, bind off all stitches as if to knit to complete 4 garter ridges with CA at end of scarf, including bind off row. Piece measures about 8½" (21 cm) from cast on.

FINISHING
Weave in ends.

POMPOMS
Using all three colors in random combinations, make 6 pompoms (see page 199) about 2½" (6.5 cm) in diameter. Using pompom tails, attach 3 pompoms to each short end of scarf as shown on page 20. Weave ends of pompom tails back into pompoms and trim evenly.

EMBROIDERY
Using CC and tapestry needle, embroider lines of French knots (see page 197) on either side of both CB stripes as shown, placing knots with about 3 knit stitches between each pair of knots. Do not cut CC between the knots. Instead, carry the yarn neatly along the wrong side of the scarf to the next French knot position to create lines of decorative running stitches on the wrong side of the scarf.

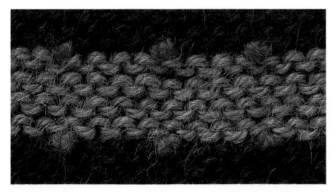

RIGHT SIDE

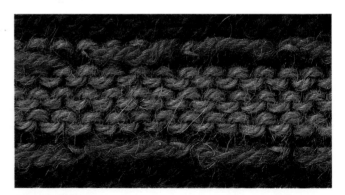

WRONG SIDE

collegiate scarf

My dad had a maroon-and-navy cashmere scarf that I discovered and borrowed when I was a teenager. It was made in the colors of his alma mater, University of Pennsylvania. I wore that scarf for years until I misplaced it somehow, somewhere. This scarf is my ode to Daddy's cashmere scarf. It is knit sideways on circular needles in garter stitch stripes. The little checks that form the center stripe are knit in two alternating colors. Choose your school's favorite colors (or those of your dad's) and throw in some contrasting colors to make your own unique version.

Plan of action: Working from the long edge makes it easy to knit a motif that runs the length of this scarf. The whole is worked back and forth in garter stitch, knitting every row.

stitches

GARTER STITCH
Knit all stitches every row.

YARN

Nashua Handknits Julia, 50% wool/ 25% mohair/25% alpaca, 93 yd (85 m)/ 1¾ oz (50 g). Yarn band gauge: 5 stitches and 6 rows = 1" (2.5 cm) in Stockinette Stitch on US 7 (4.5 mm) needles.

CA = 3983 Delphinium, 4 skeins

CB = 3961 Ladies Mantle, 1 skein

CC = 6396 Deep Blue Sea, 1 skein

CD = 4936 Blue Thyme, 1 skein

CE = 2163 Golden Honey, 1 skein

FINISHED MEASUREMENTS

60" × 9" (152.5 cm × 23 cm)

GAUGE

17 stitches and 36 rows = 4" (10 cm) in Garter Stitch.

NEEDLES

US 8 (5 mm) circular needle 29" (75 cm) long *or size you need to obtain the correct gauge*

NOTIONS

Tapestry needle

KNITTING THE SCARF

Set Up Using CA, cast on 254 stitches, taking care to make your cast on neither too loose nor too tight (see page 18).

Next Rows Knit 27 rows in Garter Stitch, ending with a wrong side row to complete 14 garter ridges, including the cast-on row.

Next Rows Change to CB and knit 4 rows.

Next Rows Change to CC and knit 4 rows. Piece measures about 4" (10 cm) from cast on.

Change to CD and CE, and work 8 rows in Checked Garter Stitch pattern as follows:

Row 1 (right side) *K2 with CD, K2 with CE; repeat from * to last 2 stitches, K2 with CD.

Row 2 (wrong side) *Bring CD to back of work, K2 with CD, bring CD to front of work, bring CE to back of work, K2 with CE, bring CE to front of work; repeat from * to last 2 stitches, bring CD to back of work, K2 with CD.

Rows 3 and 4 Repeat Rows 1 and 2 once more.

Row 5 (right side) *K2 with CE, K2 with CD; repeat from * to last 2 stitches, K2 with CE.

Row 6 (wrong side) *Bring CE to back of work, K2 with CE, bring CE to front of work, bring CD to back of work, K2 with CD, bring CD to front of work; repeat from * to last 2 stitches, bring CE to back of work, K2 with CE.

Row 7 and 8 Repeat Rows 5 and 6 once more.

Resume working Garter Stitch stripes as follows:

Rows 9–12 Change to CC and knit 4 rows.

Rows 13–16 Change to CB and knit 4 rows.

Next Rows Change to CA and knit 27 rows, ending with a right-side row.

Next Row Using CA, bind off all stitches as if to knit. This completes 14 garter ridges with CA at end of scarf, including bind-off row. Piece measures about 9" (23 cm) from cast on.

FINISHING

Weave in ends.

COLLEGIATE SCARF CHART

■ **CD BLUE THYME**

■ **CE GOLDEN HONEY**

floral and tasseled scarf
with mitered corners

easy embroidery stitches add a feminine touch to this rich, red stockinette stitch scarf, inspired by a festive Mexican folk costume that is often decorated with intricate embroidery. Two easy embroidery stitches are all you'll need to create the swingy floral vine. The striped and mitered edges finish the scarf off neatly, and the tassels give it a festive look. I've included directions for both a long and a short version.

Plan of action: First you knit back and forth for the body of the scarf and then you work the mitered edge around the outside of it. Edging is worked in the round, picking up stitches from all four sides of the scarf. Stitches are divided onto two circular needles, and worked using the third needle. You may find it helpful to use a different colored marker to indicate the beginning of the round. Finally you add the decorative embroidery and the tassels.

stitches

STOCKINETTE STITCH
Knit all stitches on right side rows, and purl all stitches on wrong side rows.

YARN
Nashua Handknits Julia, 50% wool/25% mohair/25% alpaca, 93 yd (85 m)/1¾ oz (50 g). Yarn band gauge: 5 stitches and 6 rows = 1" (2.5 cm) in Stockinette Stitch on US 7 (4.5 mm) needles.

CA = 6085 Geranium, 4 skeins for short version; 5 skeins for long version

CB = 6086 Velvet Moss, 2 skeins for both versions

CC = 2163 Golden Honey, 1 skein for both versions

SIZES AND FINISHED MEASUREMENTS
Short version, 60" × 8" (152.5 cm × 20.5 cm)

Long version, 75" × 8" (190.5 cm × 20.5 cm). Model shown is long version.

GAUGE
16 stitches and 21 rows = 4" (10 cm) in Stockinette Stitch.

NEEDLES
Three US 9 (5.5 mm) circular needles 29" (75 cm) long *or size you need to obtain the correct gauge*

NOTIONS
Tapestry needle

Stitch markers

Scrap cardboard 4" or 5" (10 cm or 12.5 cm) square for making tassels

ABBREVIATIONS
M1 = make one stitch using the backward loop method (see page 200).

KNITTING THE SCARF	SHORT VERSION	LONG VERSION
Set Up Using CA and taking care to make your cast on neither too loose nor too tight (see page 18), cast on	220 sts	280 sts

Next Rows Work in Stockinette Stitch back and forth in rows until piece measures 5" (12.5 cm) from cast on, ending with a right side row. Do not break yarn.

Round 1: Set Up for Mitered Edging Using CB and a different circular needle from the one holding the scarf stitches, and with right side still facing, place marker, pick up and knit 1 stitch in corner of scarf, place marker, pick up and knit 25 stitches along short side of scarf (about 1 stitch for every row; the short end will flare slightly because of the difference between the stitch and row gauges), place marker, pick up 1 stitch in corner, place marker. With the same circular needle, pick up and knit along the cast on edge of scarf.

Using the third circular needle, place marker, pick up and knit 1 stitch in corner of scarf, place marker, pick up and knit 25 stitches along short side of scarf, place marker, pick up 1 stitch in corner, place marker. With the same circular needle, knit across from the original scarf needle.

	SHORT VERSION	LONG VERSION
You now have	494 sts	614 sts

Round 2 *K1 (corner stitch), M1 (see page 200), purl to next corner stitch, M1; repeat from * 3 more times.

You now have	502 sts	622 sts

Round 3 Work even, knitting each of the 4 corner stitches as you come to them, and purling the remaining stitches of the round.

Round 4 Change to CC. *K1 (corner stitch), M1, knit to next corner stitch, M1; repeat from * 3 more times.

You now have	510 sts	630 sts

Round 5 Work even as for Round 3.

Round 6 *K1 (corner stitch), M1, purl to next corner stitch, M1; repeat from * 3 more times.

You now have	518 sts	638 sts

Round 7 Change to CA. Knit.

Round 8 Repeat Round 6.

You now have	526 sts	646 sts

Round 9 Work even as for Round 3.

Round 10 Change to CB. Repeat Round 4.

You now have	534 sts	654 sts

Round 11 Work even as for Round 3.

Round 12 Repeat Round 6.

You now have	542 sts	662 sts

Change to CA and loosely bind off all stitches as if to knit on next round.

FINISHING

Weave in ends. Block scarf lightly on a flat surface such as a carpet or bed.

EMBROIDERY

Using a single strand of CB, embroider a gently curving line of chain stitch (see page 197) along the center of the stockinette section of the scarf. With single strand of CB, work leaves along each side of the curving line using a large individual chain stitch for each leaf. Using a single strand of CC, embroider randomly placed 3-petal lazy daisies (see page 197) at end of some of the leaves. Using a double strand of CC, work a French knot (see page 197 in the center of each flower.

TASSELS

Using all three colors in random combinations, make four tassels (see page 199) about 4" or 5" (10 cm or 12.5 cm) long. If desired, trim the cardboard after every one or two tassels to make them different sizes. Use a 20" (51 cm) double strand of yarn for the top of each tassel's "head", and wrap the "neck" of each tassel using a double strand of yarn in two different colors. Braid the strands from the tassel heads as shown, and secure the end of each braid with an overhand knot. Tie a tassel to each corner of scarf. Weave in ends of braids on wrong side of scarf.

Chain-stitched vine, with lazy daisy accents.

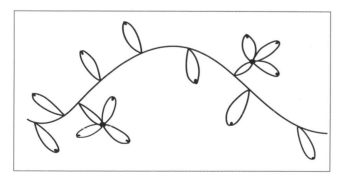

Section of vine, to be enlarged.

Attaching the tassel.

coleus
scarf

every summer I grow many kinds of coleus in large pots on my patio. I love their colors and the intricate shapes and patterns of their leaves. This striped and patterned scarf is knit in the round, using those same beautiful colors, then steeked, magically creating the fringe. After the scarf is complete, generous-size French knots decorate the Fair Isle pattern to make the design even more eye-catching.

Plan of action: The scarf is worked in the round with the cast-on and bind-off edges forming the long sides of the scarf when finished. After you complete the knitting, you will cut the scarf open, so that the sides of the cut become the short ends of the scarf. You then unravel both of the short ends to create the fringe. For the Coleus design see the instructions on pages 191 and 195 on following a chart.

stitches

REVERSE STOCKINETTE RIDGE
Round 1 Knit.
Rounds 2 and 3 Purl.

STOCKINETTE STITCH
Knit all stitches every round.

FINISHED MEASUREMENTS

54" × 9" (137 cm × 23 cm), not including fringe

GAUGE

18 stitches and 25 rows = 4" (10 cm) in pattern from Coleus Chart using larger needles.

NEEDLES

US 8 (5 mm) circular needle 29" (75 cm) long *or size you need to obtain the correct gauge*

US 7 (4.5 mm) circular needle 29" (75 cm) long

NOTIONS

Tapestry needle

Stitch markers

YARN

Nashua Handknits Julia, 50% wool/ 25% mohair/25% alpaca, 93 yd (85 m)/ 1¾ oz (50 g). Yarn band gauge: 5 stitches and 6 rows = 1" (2.5 cm) in Stockinette Stitch on US 7 (4.5 mm) needles.

CA = 5084 Zinnia Pink, 2 skeins

CB = 4345 Coleus, 3 skeins

CC = 3961 Ladies Mantle, 3 skeins

CD = 2083 Magenta, 1 skein

KNITTING THE SCARF

Note Make sure you carry the yarn not being knit with very loosely behind your work. Otherwise the Fair Isle pattern will pull in and not be the same length as the striped section of the scarf.

Set Up Using CA and smaller circular needle, cast on 260 stitches, taking care to make your cast on neither too loose nor too tight (see page 18).

Place marker and join for working in the round, being careful not to twist stitches.

Round 1 K10, place marker, P240, place marker, K10.

Note The first and last 10 stitches of every round will be knit for the remainder of the scarf in order to identify the fringe sections.

Round 2 Knit all stitches.

Round 3 K10, P240, K10.

Rounds 4 and 5 Repeat Rounds 2 and 3 once more.

Rounds 6–8 Change to CB and work 3 rounds of Reverse Stockinette Ridge.

Rounds 9–11 Change to CC and work 3 rounds of Reverse Stockinette Ridge.

Rounds 12–14 Change to CD and work 3 rounds of Reverse Stockinette Ridge.

Rounds 15–17 Change to CC and work 3 rounds of Reverse Stockinette Ridge.

Rounds 18–20 Change to CB and work 3 rounds of Reverse Stockinette Ridge.

Rounds 21–23 Change to CA and work 3 rounds of Reverse Stockinette Ridge.

Rounds 24–26 Change to CC and work Rounds 1–3 of Coleus Scarf Chart (page 33).

Rounds 27–42 Change to larger circular needle. Using colors as shown, work Rounds 4–19 of Coleus Scarf Chart.

Rounds 43–45 Change to smaller circular needle and CC. Work Rounds 20–22 of Coleus Scarf Chart.

Rounds 46–48 Change to CA and work 3 rounds of Reverse Stockinette Ridge.

Rounds 49–51 Change to CB and work 3 rounds of Reverse Stockinette Ridge.

Rounds 52–54 Change to CC and work 3 rounds of Reverse Stockinette Ridge.

Rounds 55–57 Change to CD and work 3 rounds of Reverse Stockinette Ridge.

Rounds 58–60 Change to CC and work 3 rounds of Reverse Stockinette Ridge.

Rounds 61–63 Change to CB and work 3 rounds of Reverse Stockinette Ridge.

Round 64 Change to CA. Knit all stitches.

Round 65 K10, P240, K10.

Rounds 66–69 Repeat Rounds 64 and 65 twice.

Bind off all stitches, matching the amount of stretch along cast-on edge so the long sides of the scarf will be even.

FRINGE

With sharp scissors, cut the scarf open along the center of the 20 fringe stitches; do not cut near the pattern areas.

Using a knitting needle or tapestry needle and beginning at the bind-off edge, carefully unravel 5 rounds of stitches from the 10-stitch stockinette fringe section at each end of scarf. Tie each bundle of unraveled ends with an overhand knot, snug against the end of the charted pattern as shown on page 36. Continue in this manner until all unraveled tails have been knotted into 5-round fringe bundles at each end of scarf.

FINISHING

Weave in ends. Spritz scarf with water, especially the kinked strands of fringe. Steam scarf to even out the charted colorwork section and straighten the fringe. Alternatively, hand wash the scarf according to the label instructions and dry flat, smoothing the colorwork section and fringe by hand.

EMBROIDERY

Using a double strand of CA and beginning at one end of scarf, embroider a ring of French knots (see page 197) around the inner edge of the first complete coleus motif as shown.

Using a double strand of CD, embroider a ring of French knots around the inside of the next complete coleus motif.

Embroider the rest of the coleus motifs in this manner, alternating between CA and CD as shown.

Using CD, embroider a half-circle of French knots around the partial inner circle of each half-motif at ends of scarf.

Alternate-color French knots encircle each coleus motif.

COLEUS SCARF CHART

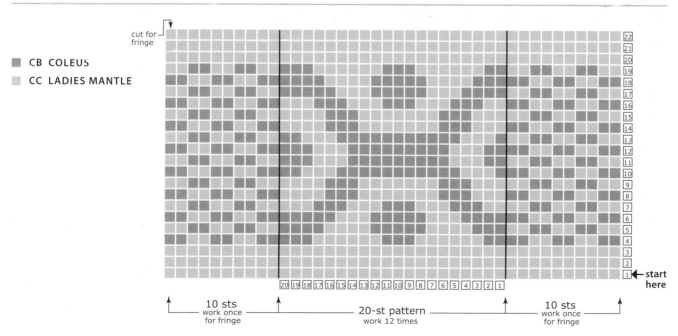

CB COLEUS
CC LADIES MANTLE

10 sts
work once
for fringe

20-st pattern
work 12 times

10 sts
work once
for fringe

start here

navajo-
inspired
afghan

An afghan or throw is just a giant scarf. It's a time commitment, but you can work on it for several years if you're not in a hurry. For this project, I enlarged the Coleus Scarf (page 30) concept to create a throw. It features a diamond pattern that is relatively easy to knit once you establish the pattern over the first few rows. The Fair Isle panels are separated with rows of garter stitch to make the throw lie flat and to give it a look similar to a Navajo blanket. Although this throw will take a while to complete, it will keep you warm while you're knitting it and it will keep your family warm as they snuggle under it for decades after.

Plan of action: The afghan is worked in the round with the cast-on and bind-off edges forming the short sides of the afghan when finished. After the knitting is complete, the afghan is cut open, and the sides of the cut become the long ends of the afghan. Stitches are unraveled along each of the long ends to create the fringe as for the Coleus Scarf (see page 33). See pages 191 and 195 for instructions on working from a chart.

YARN

Nashua Handknits Julia, 50% wool/ 25% mohair/25% alpaca, 93 yd (85 m)/ 1¾ oz (50 g). Yarn band gauge: 5 stitches and 6 rows = 1" (2.5 cm) in Stockinette Stitch on US 7 (4.5 mm) needles.

CA = 8118 Espresso, 11 skeins
CB = 2250 French Pumpkin, 7 skeins
CC = 8141 Pretty Pink, 6 skeins
CD = 5185 Spring Green, 6 skeins
CE = 4936 Blue Thyme, 6 skeins
CF = 2230 Rock Henna, 4 skeins

FINISHED MEASUREMENTS

53" × 70" (134.5 cm × 178 cm), not including fringe

GAUGE

19 stitches and 21 rounds = 4" (10 cm) in stockinette pattern from Diamond Chart using larger needles. 19 stitches and 26½ rounds = 4" (10 cm) in Garter Stitch using smaller needles.

NEEDLES

US 8 (5 mm) circular needle 29" (75 cm) long *or size you need to obtain the correct gauge*

US 7 (4.5 mm) circular needle 29" (75 cm) long *or size you need to obtain the correct gauge*

NOTIONS

Tapestry needle

Stitch markers

stitches

GARTER STITCH
Round 1 Knit.
Round 2 Purl.
Repeat these 2 rounds for pattern.

STOCKINETTE STITCH
Knit all stitches every round.

STRIPE PATTERN
Round 1 With CE, knit.
Round 2 With CE, purl.
Rounds 3–6 Repeat Rounds 1 and 2 two more times: 3 Garter Ridges completed with CE.

Rounds 7–10 With CF, repeat Rounds 1 and 2 two times: 2 Garter Ridges completed with CF.
Rounds 11–14 With CD, repeat Rounds 1 and 2 two times: 2 Garter Ridges completed with CD.
Rounds 15–18 With CC, repeat Rounds 1 and 2 two times: 2 Garter Ridges completed with CB.
Rounds 19–22 With CA, repeat Rounds 1 and 2 two times: 2 Garter Ridges completed with CA.

Rounds 23–26 With CB, repeat Rounds 1 and 2 two times: 2 Garter Ridges completed with CC.
Rounds 27–30 With CD, repeat Rounds 1 and 2 two times: 2 Garter Ridges completed with CD.
Rounds 31–34 With CF, repeat Rounds 1 and 2 two times: 2 Garter Ridges completed with CF.
Rounds 35–40 With CE, repeat Rounds 1–6: 3 Garter Ridges completed with CE; 20 total Garter Ridges completed from beginning of Stripe pattern. Repeat Rounds 1–40 for pattern.

KNITTING THE AFGHAN

Set Up and Round 1 Using CE and smaller circular needle, cast on 273 stitches, taking care to make your cast on neither too loose nor too tight (see page 18). The cast on counts as Round 1 of Stripe pattern. Place marker and join for working in the round, being careful not to twist stitches.

Round 2 K10, place marker, P253, place marker, K10.

Note The first and last 10 stitches of every round are knit for the remainder of the afghan in order to identify the fringe sections.

Rounds 3–40 Work Rounds 3–40 of Stripe pattern on center 253 stitches, keeping 10 stitches at each end of round in Stockinette Stitch for fringe section.

Rounds 41–75 Change to larger circular needle. With CB for background color, work Rounds 1–35 of Navajo-Inspired Afghan Chart in Stockinette Stitch using CB and CA.

Rounds 76–115 Change to smaller circular needle. Work Rounds 1–40 of Stripe pattern, keeping 10 stitches at each end of round in Stockinette Stitch for fringe section.

Rounds 116–150 Change to larger circular needle. With CC for background color, work Rounds 1–35 of Navajo-Inspired Afghan Chart in Stockinette Stitch using CC and CA.

Rounds 151–190 Change to smaller circular needle. Work Rounds 1–40 of Stripe pattern, keeping 10 stitches at each end of round in Stockinette Stitch for fringe section.

Rounds 191–340 Repeat Rounds 41–190 once more.

Rounds 341–415 Repeat Rounds 41–115 once more.

Bind off all stitches, matching the amount of stretch in cast-on edge so the short sides of the afghan will be even.

FRINGE

With sharp scissors, cut the afghan open along the beginning of the round, exactly in the center of the 21 stitches outside the diamond pattern area (labelled on the chart as "for fringe").

Using a knitting needle or tapestry needle and beginning at the bind-off edge, carefully unravel 4 rounds of stitches from the 10-stitch stockinette fringe section at each end of afghan. Tie each bundle of unraveled ends with an overhand knot, snug against the end of the charted pattern as shown.

Continue in this manner until all unraveled tails have been knotted into 4-round fringe bundles at each end of afghan.

Unravelling the knitting and knotting the fringe.

NAVAJO-INSPIRED AFGHAN CHART

■ CA ESPRESSO

■ CB FRENCH PUMPKIN OR
CC PRETTY PINK
(SEE INSTRUCTIONS)

cut for
fringe

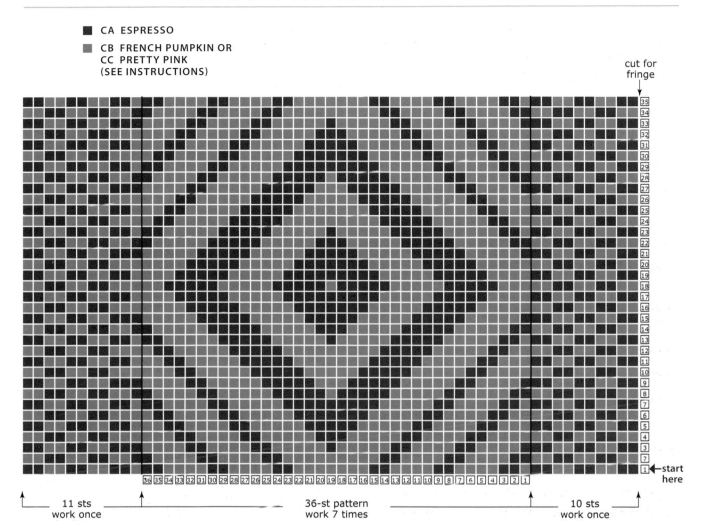

← start
here

11 sts
work once
for fringe

36-st pattern
work 7 times

10 sts
work once
for fringe

EMBROIDERY

Note Work loosely so the embroidery stitches do not distort the knitted fabric.

Using a single strand of CD or CE, use chain stitch (see page 197) to embroider an outline around the outer edge of each large diamond motif, alternating colors for each diamond as shown.

Using the opposite color from the one used to outline the large diamond, work chain stitch in the same manner around the small diamond motif in the center of each large diamond.

FINISHING

Weave in ends. Spritz afghan with water, especially the kinked strands of fringe. Steam afghan to even out the charted colorwork sections and straighten the fringe. Alternatively, hand wash the afghan according to the yarn label instructions and dry flat, smoothing the colorwork section and fringe by hand.

Spring Green and Blue Thyme alternate to outline the diamond motifs with chain stitch.

family inspiration

MY GRANDMOTHER Frieda Roessler Nicholas came to the United States from Germany in 1911 when she was 10 years old. She was one of thousands of immigrants who moved to America to make a better life and to take advantage of all it has to offer. Gram's life was lived as many other immigrants' were. She learned English at school, then left after eighth grade to begin working in a shirt factory, where she learned to sew men's shirts along with many of the other immigrants in Dover, New Jersey.

Soon she met and married my grandfather, Archie, an English immigrant. They had two boys — my Uncle Harry and my dad, Arch, Jr. Gram worked hard to provide for her family. The thing I remember most about Gram was that her hands were always busy. If she wasn't working at the school cafeteria, she was cooking or baking bread or stitching something at her home. She embroidered, tatted, sewed, and crocheted, as did her mother. I clearly remember every detail of her cozy home, which was filled with completed needlework projects. On the back of her couch, she always kept a giant wool throw, crocheted in stripes with giant crocheted flowers appliqueed onto it. To this day, I think no home is complete without some bit of handmade textile gracing a chair or couch.

Colorful
HATS

sister-love striped hats

i grew up in a family of five sisters. I often wonder how my mother kept everyone's clothes straight! But with the millions of possible color combinations you could explore for this easy-to-knit hat, any sisters in your family will have no trouble knowing whose hat is whose. They are super simple to knit in the round on circular needles, with no shaping! To make the hats even more playful, add polka dots in an easy embroidery stitch, along with pompoms or tassels on the square corners.

Plan of action: The hat is knit in the round as a straight cylinder without a shaped crown. After binding off, you fold the hat flat and sew across the bound-off edge to close the top.

stitches

> **GARTER STITCH**
> **Round 1** Knit.
> **Round 2** Purl.
> Repeat these two rounds for pattern.
>
> **K2, P2 RIB**
> Work all rounds as *K2, P2; repeat from * to end of round.
>
> **STOCKINETTE STITCH**
> Knit all stitches every round.

SIZES AND FINISHED CIRCUMFERENCES

Small, 17¾" (45 cm); Medium, 19½" (49.5 cm); Large, 20½" (52 cm)

Both models shown in size medium.

GAUGE

18 stitches and 26 rounds = 4" (10 cm) in Stockinette Stitch worked in the round using larger needle.

NEEDLES

US 8 (5 mm) circular needle 16" (40 cm) long *or size you need to obtain the correct gauge*

US 6 (4 mm) circular needle 16" (40 cm) long

NOTIONS

Tapestry needle

Stitch marker

Scrap cardboard for making tassels and pompoms

Pompom maker (optional)

YARN

Nashua Handknits Julia, 50% wool/ 25% mohair/25% alpaca, 93 yd (85 m)/ 1¾ oz (50 g). Yarn band gauge: 5 stitches and 6 rows = 1" (2.5 cm) in Stockinette Stitch on US 7 (4.5 mm) needles.

Version 1:

CA = 2250 French Pumpkin, 1 skein for all sizes

CB = 5185 Spring Green, 1 skein for all sizes

CC = 2083 Magenta, 1 skein for all sizes

CD = 8141 Pretty Pink, 1 skein for all sizes

Version 2:

CA = 2083 Magenta, 1 skein for all sizes

CB = 6416 Midnight Blue, 1 skein for all sizes

CC = 5185 Spring Green, 1 skein for all sizes

KNITTING VERSION 1	SMALL	MEDIUM	LARGE
Set Up Using CA and smaller circular needle, cast on	80 sts	88 sts	92 sts
Place marker and join for working in the round, being careful not to twist stitches.			
Next Rounds Beginning and ending with a purl round, work in Garter Stitch for 3 rounds.			
Next Rounds Change to CB and work in K2, P2 Rib until rib measures 1½" (3.8 cm) above last Garter Stitch round.			
Next Rounds Change to CA and work 4 rounds in Garter Stitch, beginning with a knit round and ending with a purl round.			
Change to larger circular needle and work stripe pattern as follows:			
Rounds 1 and 2 With CC, knit.			
Rounds 3 and 4 With CD, knit.			
Repeat the last 4 rounds, ending with a completed 2-round stripe, until piece measures from cast on edge	7" (18 cm)	7½" (19 cm)	8" (20.5 cm)
Next Rounds Change to CB and work 4 rounds in Garter Stitch, beginning with a knit round and ending with a purl round. Bind off all stitches on next round as if to knit.			

FINISHING

Fold hat flat with right sides together, and sew across bound-off edge to close top of hat. Weave in ends.

Stitching the top seam.

POMPOMS

Make two pompoms (see page 199) in the colors of your choice. Each of the pompoms shown uses equal amounts of two colors, one in CA and CC, and the other in CA and CD. Attach one pompom to each top corner of hat.

EMBROIDERY

Using CB, embroider about five randomly placed spider web stitch motifs (see page 198), on each side of hat, varying the sizes of the spider webs as shown.

Spider web polka dots detail.

KNITTING VERSION 2	SMALL	MEDIUM	LARGE
Set Up Using CA and smaller circular needle, cast on	80 sts	88 sts	92 sts
Place marker and join for working in the round, being careful not to twist stitches.			
Next Rounds Work in Stockinette Stitch for 6 rounds; fabric will curl up at the bottom with the purl side showing to form a rolled edge.			
Next Rounds Change to CB and work in K2, P2 Rib until rib measures 1½" (3.8 cm) above last row of rolled edge.			
Next Rounds Change to CA and work 4 rounds in Garter Stitch, beginning with a knit round and ending with a purl round.			
Change to larger circular needle and work stripe pattern as follows:			
Rounds 1–6 With CC, knit.			
Rounds 7–12 With CB, knit.			
Repeat the last 12 rounds	1 time	1 time	2 times
Work Rounds 1–6 only	1 time	1 time	0 times
You now have	5 stripes	5 stripes	6 stripes
Piece measures from cast-on edge about	7" (18 cm)	7" (18 cm)	8" (20.5 cm)
Next Rounds Change to CA and work 4 rounds in Garter Stitch, beginning with a knit round and ending with a purl round. Bind off all stitches on next round as if to knit.			

FINISHING

If desired, tack rolled lower edge of hat in place using CA. Fold hat flat and sew across bound-off edge (see facing page) to close top of hat. Bring the two top corners of the hat together and sew together securely. Weave in ends.

TASSELS

Using CA, make two tassels (see page 199) about 4" or 5" (10 cm or 12.5 cm) long. Use a 20" (51 cm) double strand of yarn for the top of each tassel's "head." Braid the strands from the tassel heads for about 4" or 5" (10 or 12.5 cm), and secure the end of each braid with an overhand knot. Tie tassels to hat where the top corners of hat meet. Weave in ends of braids on wrong side of hat.

Attaching the tassel.

the twins' beanies

like twins, no beanie is truly quite alike. Reverse stockinette stitch stripes allow lots of room for creative interpretation of a theme. The beanie at the left (version 1) uses five different colors while the beanie at the right (version 2) uses only three colors. The finishing is the same on both, with French knots worked along the decrease stitches of the crown, creating an interesting pie-like pattern. Pompoms can either dangle from a braid or be attached firmly at the top, reminiscent of a Scottish toque often worn with a kilt.

Plan of action: Both versions of the hat are worked in the round on circular needles changing to double pointed needles when there are too few stitches to fit comfortably. The crown is shaped with double decreases creating distinctive lines which radiate up to the peak.

stitches

REVERSE STOCKINETTE RIDGES
Round 1 Knit.
Rounds 2 and 3 Purl.
Repeat these three rounds for pattern.

STOCKINETTE STITCH
Knit all stitches every round.

DOUBLE DECREASE
Slip the next 2 stitches as if to knit 2 together, K1, pass the 2 slipped sts over: 2 stitches decreased.

YARN

Nashua Handknits Julia, 50% wool/ 25% mohair/25% alpaca, 93 yd (85 m)/ 1¾ oz (50 g). Yarn band gauge: 5 stitches and 6 rows = 1" (2.5 cm) in Stockinette Stitch on US 7 (4.5 mm) needles.

Version 1:

CA = 8118 Espresso, 1 skein for all sizes
CB = 6085 Geranium, 1 skein for all sizes
CC = 2163 Golden Honey, 1 skein for all sizes
CD = 3983 Delphinium, 1 skein for all sizes
CE = 2250 French Pumpkin, 1 skein for all sizes

Version 2:

CA = 3961 Ladies Mantle, 1 skein for all sizes
CB = 0178 Harvest Spice, 1 skein for all sizes
CC = 3983 Delphinium, 1 skein for all sizes

SIZES AND FINISHED CIRCUMFERENCES

Small, 20" (51 cm); Medium, 21¼" (54 cm); Large, 22½" (57 cm)

Models shown are large (version 1) and medium (version 2).

GAUGE

16 stitches and 24 rounds = 4" (10 cm) in Reverse Stockinette Ridges worked in the round using larger needle.

NEEDLES

US 8 (5 mm) circular needle 16" (40 cm) long *or size you need to obtain the correct gauge*

Set of four or five US 8 (5 mm) double-pointed needles *or size you need to obtain the correct gauge*

US 6 (4 mm) circular needle 16" (40 cm) long

NOTIONS

Tapestry needle

Stitch marker

ABBREVIATIONS

K2tog = knit 2 stitches together

KNITTING VERSION 1	SMALL	MEDIUM	LARGE

Brim

Set Up Using CA and smaller circular needle, cast on

	SMALL	MEDIUM	LARGE
	80 sts	85 sts	90 sts

Place marker and join for working in the round, being careful not to twist stitches.

Next Rounds With CA, purl 2 rounds.

Next Rounds Change to Reverse Stockinette Ridges pattern. Work 3 rounds each in the following colors in this order: CB, CC, CD, CE.

Next Rounds Change to larger circular needle. Continue in Reverse Stockinette Ridges pattern, and work 3 rounds each in the following colors in this order: CA, CB, CC, CD.

You now have 9 Reverse Stockinette Ridges, including the ridge formed by purling the first 2 rounds with CA.

Next Rounds Work in Reverse Stockinette Ridges pattern

	SMALL	MEDIUM	LARGE
Next Rounds Work in Reverse Stockinette Ridges pattern	0 more ridges	1 more ridge in CE	2 more ridges in CE and CA
You now have	9 ridges	10 ridges	11 ridges
Piece measures from cast on about	3¼" (8.5 cm)	3¾" (9.5 cm)	4¼" (11 cm)

Crown

Note Change to double-pointed needles when there are too few stitches to fit comfortably around the circular needle.

Change to CA and continue in Stockinette Stitch.

Round 1 Knit.

Round 2

Small only: *K7, Double Decrease, K6; repeat from * to end.

Medium only: *K7, Double Decrease, K7; repeat from * to end.

Large only: *K8, Double Decrease, K7; repeat from * to end.

You now have	SMALL	MEDIUM	LARGE
	70 sts	75 sts	80 sts

Round 3 Knit.

Round 4

Small only: *K6, Double Decrease, K5; repeat from * to end.

Medium only: *K6, Double Decrease, K6; repeat from * to end.

Large only: *K7, Double Decrease, K6; repeat from * to end.

You now have	SMALL	MEDIUM	LARGE
	60 sts	65 sts	70 sts

Round 5 Knit.

Round 6

Small only: *K5, Double Decrease, K4; repeat from * to end.

Medium only: *K5, Double Decrease, K5; repeat from * to end.

Large only: *K6, Double Decrease, K5; repeat from * to end.

You now have	50 sts	55 sts	60 sts

Round 7 Knit.

Round 8

Small only: *K4, Double Decrease, K3; repeat from * to end.

Medium only: *K4, Double Decrease, K4; repeat from * to end.

Large only: *K5, Double Decrease, K4; repeat from * to end.

You now have	40 sts	45 sts	50 sts

Round 9 Knit.

Round 10

Small only: *K3, Double Decrease, K2; repeat from * to end.

Medium only: *K3, Double Decrease, K3; repeat from * to end.

Large only: *K4, Double Decrease, K3; repeat from * to end.

You now have	30 sts	35 sts	40 sts

Round 11 Knit.

Round 12

Small only: *K2, Double Decrease, K1; repeat from * to end.

Medium only: *K2, Double Decrease, K2; repeat from * to end.

Large only: *K3, Double Decrease, K2; repeat from * to end.

You now have	20 sts	25 sts	30 sts

Round 13 Knit.

Round 14

Small only: *K1, Double Decrease; repeat from * to end.

Medium only: *K1, Double Decrease, K1; repeat from * to end.

Large only: *K2, Double Decrease, K1; repeat from * to end.

You now have	10 sts	15 sts	20 sts

Round 15 Knit.

Round 16

Small only: *K2tog; repeat from * to end.

Medium only: *K2tog; repeat from * to last st, K1.

Large only: *K1, Double Decrease; repeat from * to end.

You now have	5 sts	8 sts	10 sts

Medium and Large only: Work 1 round as *K2tog; repeat from * to end.

You now have	5 sts	4 sts	5 sts

FINISHING

Cut yarn leaving a 10" (25.5 cm) tail. Thread tail on tapestry needle and run through all stitches like a drawstring. Pull tail firmly to close top of hat, and weave in tail on wrong side. Weave in remaining ends.

POMPOMS

Make three pompoms (see page 199), one each in CC, CD, and CE, and leaving 12" (30.5 cm) long ties for each pompom. Braid the three ties together as shown and secure end of braid with an overhand knot. Attach braid to top of hat and weave in ends of braid on wrong side of hat.

EMBROIDERY

Using a double strand of CC, embroider French knots (see page 197) along the decrease lines of crown as shown.

yarn journeys

THE FIRST TIME I knit, I was eight years old and taking a car trip to Kentucky. I distinctly remember the orange-and-yellow garter stitch bag I knit in very thick cotton yarn. After that introduction to knitting, my grandmother taught me to crochet, and I spent several years making crocheted ponchos and other projects. When I was in high school, I sewed almost 100 percent of my wardrobe. Through sewing I discovered my love of color and fabric, and I dreamed that I would one be a famous clothing designer.

In college, I studied textiles and clothing, but I found myself with time on my hands traveling to and from classes. A sewing machine wasn't an option on public transportation, but knitting was portable — and intriguing! I was in those magical college years, discovering myself and continuing to dream of what I wanted to become. I decided I should become a knitter, among many other things. For my first sweater, I followed a pattern, but after that, I began designing my own.

I've carried my knitting with me through the years since college. Now, over twenty years later, I'm still intrigued by all the possibilities two sticks and a length of string hold. When I'm feeling intrepid, I teach myself a new technique. When I just need comfort or want to keep my hands busy, I pick up an easy project and while away the hours. Most of all, I find I never want to be without my knitting. What if I get stuck with a few minutes to spare? I could be knitting! My knitting has become my adult security blanket, and not a bad one at that.

KNITTING VERSION 2	SMALL	MEDIUM	LARGE
Brim			
Set Up Using CA and smaller circular needle, cast on	80 sts	85 sts	90 sts
Place marker and join for working in the round, being careful not to twist stitches.			
Next Rounds With CA, purl 2 rounds.			
Next Rounds Change to Reverse Stockinette Ridges pattern. Work 3 rounds each in the following colors in this order: CB, CC, CA, CB.			
Next Rounds Change to larger circular needle. Continue in Reverse Stockinette Ridges pattern, and work 3 rounds each in the following colors in this order: CC, CA, CB, CC.			
You now have 9 Reverse Stockinette Ridges, including the ridge formed by purling the first 2 rounds with CA.			
Next Rounds Work in Reverse Stockinette Ridges pattern	0 more ridges	1 more ridge using CA	2 more ridges using CA and CB
You now have	9 ridges	10 ridges	11 ridges
Piece measures from cast on about	3¼" (8.5 cm)	3¾" (9.5 cm)	4¼" (11 cm)
Crown			
Note Change to double-pointed needles when there are too few stitches to fit comfortably around the circular needle.			
Change to CB. Work crown shaping as for Version 1. *You now have*	5 sts	4 sts	5 sts

FINISHING

Cut yarn leaving a 10" (25.5 cm) tail. Thread tail on tapestry needle and run through all stitches like a drawstring. Pull tail firmly to close top of hat, and weave in tail on wrong side. Weave in remaining ends.

POMPOM

Make one pompom (see page 199) using CC. Attach pompom to top of hat.

EMBROIDERY

Using a single strand of CC, embroider French knots (see page 197) along the decrease lines of crown as for Version 1.

French knots worked along decrease lines on crown.

kaleidoscope cap

The melding of many techniques makes this hat something of a challenge but worth the effort. Although the finished hat is completely colorful and intricate looking, no more than two colors are used when knitting any round. The magic is in the finishing, which includes duplicate stitch and two simple embroidery stitches.

Plan of action: This intricate hat starts with a bobble edging, works a Five-Color Garter Stitch pattern set off by Reverse Stockinette Ridges and proceeds to follow charts for the diamonds in the body of the hat and the crown. (See pages 191 and 195 for instructions on following a chart.) The decreases which shape the crown are worked in two colors and become part of the pattern — creating the kaleidoscope appearance of the top shaping. The additional colors are added after completion by working embroidery stitches including duplicate stitch, cross stitch, and French knots.

YARN

Nashua Handknits Julia, 50% wool/ 25% mohair/25% alpaca, 93 yd (85 m)/ 1¾ oz (50 g). Yarn band gauge: 5 stitches and 6 rows = 1" (2.5 cm) in Stockinette Stitch on US 7 (4.5 mm) needles.

CA = 5084 Zinnia Pink, 1 skein for both sizes

CB = 6086 Velvet Moss, 1 skein for both sizes

CC = 5185 Spring Green, 1 skein for both sizes

CD = 2163 Golden Honey, 1 skein for both sizes

CE = 0178 Harvest Spice, 1 skein for both sizes

SIZES AND FINISHED CIRCUMFERENCES

Small, 17" (43 cm); Medium, 20½" (51.5 cm)

Model shown in size medium.

GAUGE

20 stitches and 21 rounds = 4" (10 cm) in Stockinette Stitch colorwork pattern from chart worked in the round using larger needle.

NEEDLES

US 7 (4.5 mm) circular needle 16" (40 cm) long *or size you need to obtain the correct gauge*

Set of four or five US 7 (4.5 mm) double-pointed needles *or size you need to obtain the correct gauge*

US 5 (3.75 mm) circular needle 16" (40 cm) long

NOTIONS

Tapestry needle

Stitch marker

ABBREVIATIONS

K2tog = knit 2 stitches together

ssk = slip, slip, knit these 2 stitches together

stitches

BOBBLE EDGING
*P5, (K1, P1, K1, P1) all in same st to increase 1 st to 4 sts, turn work so wrong side is facing, K4 bobble sts, turn work so right side is facing, P4 bobble sts, pass second, third, and fourth sts on right needle over first st to decrease bobble back to 1 st; rep from * to end of round.

FIVE-COLOR GARTER STITCH
(MULTIPLE OF 6 STITCHES)
Round 1 *K3 with CB, K3 with CC; repeat from * to end.
Round 2 *Bring CB to front of work, P3 with CB, bring CB to back of work,

bring CC to front of work, P3 with CC, bring CC to back of work; repeat from * to end.
Round 3 *K3 with CD, K3 with CE; repeat from * to end.
Round 4 *Bring CD to front of work, P3 with CD, bring CD to back of work, bring CE to front of work, P3 with CE, bring CE to back of work; repeat from * to end.
Round 5 *K3 with CA, K3 with CB; repeat from * to end.
Round 6 *Bring CA to front of work, P3 with CA, bring CA to back of work, bring CB to front of work, P3 with CB,

bring CB to back of work; repeat from * to end.
Round 7 *K3 with CD, K3 with CC; repeat from * to end.
Round 8 *Bring CD to front of work, P3 with CD, bring CD to back of work, bring CC to front of work, P3 with CC, bring CC to back of work; repeat from * to end.

REVERSE STOCKINETTE RIDGE
Round 1 Knit.
Rounds 2 and 3 Purl.

STOCKINETTE STITCH
Knit all stitches every round.

KNITTING THE BRIM	SMALL	MEDIUM
Set Up Using CA and smaller circular needle, cast on	84 sts	102 sts
Place marker and join for working in the round, being careful not to twist stitches.		
Next Round Work Bobble Edging.		
Next Rounds Work Five-Color Garter Stitch pattern, beginning with Round 1 and ending with	Round 6	Round 8
Next 3 Rounds Change to CE. Work 1 Reverse Stockinette Ridge, increasing in last round	1 st	0 sts
You now have	85 sts	102 sts
KNITTING THE LOWER HAT AND CROWN		
Note If a color is not used for 5 or more stitches in the charted section, twist the unused color together with the working color to catch it against the back of the fabric. Change to double-pointed needles when there are too few stitches to fit comfortably around the circular needle.		
Next Rounds Change to larger circular needle. Work in pattern from Kaleidoscope Cap Chart, beginning with	Round 12	Round 1
Continue in pattern, decreasing as shown on chart, until Round 34 has been completed for both sizes.		
You now have	15 sts	18 sts
Next Round Change to CD and work for your size as follows:		
Small only: *K2tog; repeat from * to last stitch, K1.		
Medium only: *K2tog; repeat from * to end.		
You now have	8 sts	9 sts
Cut yarn leaving a 10" (25.5 cm) tail. Thread tail on tapestry needle and run through all stitches like a drawstring. Pull tail firmly to close top of hat, and weave in tail on wrong side. Weave in all loose ends.		

EMBROIDERY

Using a single strand of CD, work duplicate stitch embroidery (see page 194) around the inner edge of each large diamond as shown on embroidery chart.

Using a single strand of CC, work duplicate stitch around the outer edge of each large diamond.

Using a single strand of CE, work duplicate stitch along the middle of the zigzag line in Rounds 24–27 as shown on chart.

Using a single strand of CD, work a cross stitch in the center of each small diamond as shown on chart.

Duplicate stitch and cross stitch around and within motifs.

Using a single strand of CA, work a French knot (see page 197) in the middle of each CD pair of stitches in Round 29 as shown on chart.

Using a single strand of CE, work a French knot in the middle of each CD pair of stitches in Round 33 as shown on chart.

French knots at crown.

KALEIDOSCOPE CAP CHARTS

■	CA ZINNIA PINK	■ CD GOLDEN HONEY	◨	K2TOG WITH COLOR SHOWN
■	CB VELVET MOSS	■ CE HARVEST SPICE	◩	SSK WITH COLOR SHOWN
■	CC SPRING GREEN		○	FRENCH KNOT

KNITTING

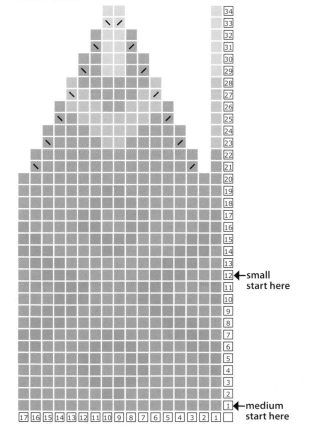

EMBROIDERY

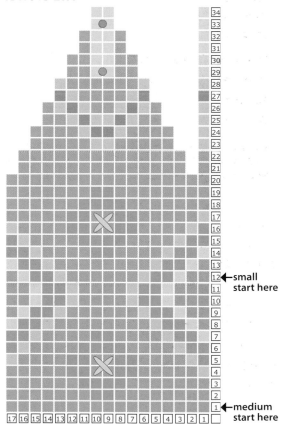

bull's eye

I love designing with concentric circles, but they don't come easily in knitting. Fair Isle circles are never *quite* round because knit stitches line up in rows and columns, creating squared-off figures in motifs. By tracing around the inside and/or outside of these motifs with embroidery, however, you can round them off to create circles and other rounded shapes. The circles around the bottom of the hat are echoed by the concentric circles that form as you shape the crown. I've used four distinct colors of yarn and knit them in Reverse Stockinette Stitch Ridges to make the increasingly smaller circles. The decreases that create the shaping are made in the "ditch" round of the pattern so they almost disappear.

Plan of action: The brim is defined by Reverse Stockinette Ridges that border both a Two-Color Garter Stitch section and the circle pattern from the chart. (See pages 191 and 195 for instructions on following a chart.) Some shaping is achieved by changing needle sizes and then single decreases create the flat crown. Afterward chain stitch embroidery enhances the circles.

stitches

REVERSE STOCKINETTE RIDGE
Round 1 Knit.
Rounds 2 and 3 Purl.

STOCKINETTE STITCH
Knit all stitches every round.

TWO-COLOR GARTER STITCH
(MULTIPLE OF 6 STITCHES)
Round 1 *K3 with CB, K3 with CC; repeat from * to end.
Round 2 *Bring CB to front of work, P3 with CB, bring CB to back of work, bring CC to front of work, P3 with CC, bring CC to back of work; repeat from * to end.
Round 3 *K3 with CC, K3 with CB; repeat from * to end.
Round 4 *Bring CC to front of work, P3 with CC, bring CC to back of work, bring CB to front of work, P3 with CB, bring CB to back of work; repeat from * to end.

YARN

Nashua Handknits Julia, 50% wool/25% mohair/25% alpaca, 93 yd (85 m)/1¾ (50 g). Yarn band gauge: 5 stitches and 6 rows = 1" (2.5 cm) in Stockinette Stitch on US 7 (4.5 mm) needles.

CA = 5084 Zinnia Pink, 1 skein for all sizes
CB = 2230 Rock Henna, 1 skein for all sizes
CC = 3961 Ladies Mantle, 1 skein for all sizes
CD = 5178 Lupine, 1 skein for all sizes

SIZES AND FINISHED CIRCUMFERENCES

Small, 18¼" (46.5 cm); Medium, 20½" (52 cm); Large, 22¾" (58 cm)
Model shown in size medium.

GAUGE

17½ stitches and 28 rounds = 4" (10 cm) in Fair Isle in Stockinette Stitch worked in the round using larger needle.

NEEDLES

US 8 (5 mm) circular needle 16" (40 cm) long *or size you need to obtain the correct gauge*

Set of four or five US 8 (5 mm) double-pointed needles *or size you need to obtain the correct gauge*

US 6 (4 mm) circular needle 16" (40 cm) long

NOTIONS

Tapestry needle
Stitch marker

ABBREVIATIONS

K2tog = knit 2 stitches together

KNITTING THE BRIM	SMALL	MEDIUM	LARGE
Set Up Using CA and smaller circular needle, cast on	78 sts	90 sts	96 sts
Place marker and join for working in the round, being careful not to twist stitches.			
Rounds 1 and 2 Purl 2 rounds. Together with the cast on, this counts as a single Reverse Stockinette Ridge.			
Rounds 3–6 Change to CB and CC. Work Rounds 1–4 of Two-Color Garter Stitch.			
Rounds 7–9 Change to CA. Work 1 Reverse Stockinette Ridge, increasing in last round	2 sts	0 sts	4 sts
You now have	80 sts	90 sts	100 sts
KNITTING THE LOWER HAT			
Note If a color is not used for 5 or more stitches in the charted section, twist the unused color together with the working color to catch it against the back of the fabric.			
Rounds 10 and 11 Change CD, and work Rounds 1–2 of Bull's Eye Chart.			
Rounds 12–19 Change to larger circular needle. Join CB and work Rounds 3–10 of Bull's Eye Chart.			
Rounds 20 and 21 Change to smaller circular needle and work Rounds 11 and 12 of Bull's Eye Chart.			
Rounds 22–24 Change to CA. Work one Reverse Stockinette Ridge.			
Rounds 25–27 Change to CC. Work one Reverse Stockinette Ridge, and in Round 27	increase 1 st	increase 0 sts	decrease 1 st
You now have	81 sts	90 sts	99 sts
KNITTING THE CROWN			
Note Change to double-pointed needles when there are too few stitches to fit comfortably around the circular needle.			
Crown is worked in Reverse Stockinette Ridge, decreasing in the first round of each ridge.			
Round 28 Change to CB.			
Small only: *K7, K2tog; repeat from * to end.			
Medium only: *K8, K2tog; repeat from * to end.			
Large only: *K9, K2tog; repeat from * to end.			
You now have	72 sts	81 sts	90 sts
Rounds 29 and 30 Purl.			

KNITTING THE CROWN (CONT'D)	SMALL	MEDIUM	LARGE
Round 31 Change to CD. *Small only:* *K6, K2tog; repeat from * to end. *Medium only:* *K7, K2tog; repeat from * to end. *Large only:* *K8, K2tog; repeat from * to end. *You now have*	63 sts	72 sts	81 sts
Rounds 32 and 33 Purl.			
Round 34 Change to CA. *Small only:* *K5, K2tog; repeat from * to end. *Medium only:* *K6, K2tog; repeat from * to end. *Large only:* *K7, K2tog; repeat from * to end. *You now have*	54 sts	63 sts	72 sts
Rounds 35 and 36 Purl.			
Round 37 Change to CC. *Small only:* *K4, K2tog; repeat from * to end. *Medium only:* *K5, K2tog; repeat from * to end. *Large only:* *K6, K2tog; repeat from * to end. *You now have*	45 sts	54 sts	63 sts
Rounds 38 and 39 Purl.			
Round 40 Change to CB. *Small only:* *K3, K2tog; repeat from * to end. *Medium only:* *K4, K2tog; repeat from * to end. *Large only:* *K5, K2tog; repeat from * to end. *You now have*	36 sts	45 sts	54 sts
Rounds 41 and 42 Purl.			
Round 43 Change to CD. *Small only:* *K2, K2tog; repeat from * to end. *Medium only:* *K3, K2tog; repeat from * to end. *Large only:* *K4, K2tog; repeat from * to end. *You now have*	27 sts	36 sts	45 sts
Rounds 44 and 45 Purl.			
Round 46 Change to CA. *Small only:* *K1, K2tog; repeat from * to end. *Medium only:* *K2, K2tog; repeat from * to end. *Large only:* *K3, K2tog; repeat from * to end. *You now have*	18 sts	27 sts	36 sts

KNITTING THE CROWN (CONT'D)	SMALL	MEDIUM	LARGE
Rounds 47 and 48 Purl.			
Round 49 Change to CC.			
Small only: *K2tog; repeat from * to end.			
Medium only: *K1, K2tog; repeat from * to end.			
Large only: *K2, K2tog; repeat from * to end.			
You now have	9 sts	18 sts	27 sts
Rounds 50 and 51 Purl.			
Small only: Go to Finishing.			
Medium and Large only: Continue as follows:			
Round 52 Change to CB.			
Medium only: *K2tog; repeat from * to end.			
Large only: *K1, K2tog; repeat from * to end.			
You now have		9 sts	18 sts
Rounds 53 and 54 Purl.			
Medium only: Go to Finishing.			
Large only: Continue as follows:			
Round 55 Change to CD. *K2tog; repeat from * to end.			
You now have			9 sts
Rounds 56 and 57 Purl.			

FINISHING

Cut yarn leaving a 10" (25.5 cm) tail. Thread tail on tapestry needle and run through all stitches like a drawstring. Pull tail firmly to close top of hat, and weave in tail on wrong side. Weave in ends.

EMBROIDERY

Using a single strand of either CA or CC chosen at random, work chain stitch embroidery (see page 197) around the outside of each knitted circle as shown, working in a smooth line to round the outline of the circle. Using a single strand of CC or CA (the opposite color from the one you used outside the circle), work chain stitch embroidery around the inside edge of each knitted circle as shown in photo on page 57.

BULL'S EYE CHART

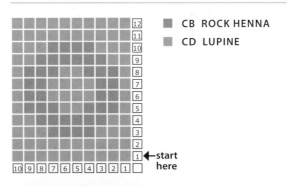

■ CB ROCK HENNA
■ CD LUPINE

←start here

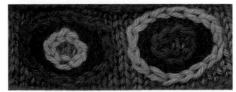

Alternate-color chain stitch around and within circular motifs.

waves and tassels

This knit-in-the-round hat is a perfect project for a knitter who's just learning the Fair Isle technique. Although the finished hat looks completely colorful, the Fair Isle wave pattern needs to be followed for only four rounds. After the hat is finished, three simple embroidery stitches (running and chain stitch and French knots) make it look much more complex than it really is. Only the knitter needs to know! The multi-colored tassels and braids give the hat a fun-loving air.

Plan of action: Worked in the round, this hat uses K2, P2 ribbing for a snug brim and then changes to larger needles and stockinette stitch for the lower hat. The wave pattern is read from the Fair Isle chart before shaping for the crown. (See pages 191 and 195 for instructions on following a chart.) The hat is then decorated with several different embroidery stitches and three different colored tassels.

stitches

> **K2, P2 RIB**
> Work all rounds as *K2, P2; repeat from * to end of round.
>
> **STOCKINETTE STITCH**
> Knit all stitches every round.

YARN

Nashua Handknits Julia, 50% wool/ 25% mohair/25% alpaca, 93 yd (85 m)/ 1¾ oz (50 g). Yarn band gauge: 5 stitches and 6 rows = 1" (2.5 cm) in Stockinette Stitch on US 7 (4.5 mm) needles.

CA = 6396 Deep Blue Sea, 1 skein for all sizes

CB = 5084 Zinnia Pink, 1 skein for all sizes

CC = 4936 Blue Thyme, 1 skein for all sizes

CD = 3961 Ladies Mantle, 1 skein for all sizes

CE = 2230 Rock Henna, 1 skein for all sizes

SIZES AND FINISHED CIRCUMFERENCES

Small, 17¾" (45 cm); Medium, 19½" (49.5 cm); Large, 21¼" (54 cm)

Model shown in size small.

GAUGE

18 stitches and 25 rounds = 4" (10 cm) in Stockinette Stitch worked in the round using larger needle.

NEEDLES

US 8 (5 mm) circular needle 16" (40 cm) long *or size you need to obtain the correct gauge*

Set of four or five US 8 (5 mm) double-pointed needles *or size you need to obtain the correct gauge*

US 7 (4.5 mm) circular needle 16" (40 cm) long

NOTIONS

Tapestry needle

Stitch marker

Scrap cardboard for making tassels

ABBREVIATIONS

K2tog = knit 2 stitches together

KNITTING THE BRIM	SMALL	MEDIUM	LARGE
Set Up Using CA and smaller circular needle, cast on	76 sts	84 sts	92 sts
Place marker and join for working in the round, being careful not to twist stitches.			
Next Round Purl.			
Next Round Change to CB and knit 1 round.			
Next Rounds Work in K2, P2 Rib until piece measures 1½" (3.8 cm) from cast-on edge.			
Next Round Change to larger circular needle. Knit 1 round, increasing 4 sts evenly.			
You now have	80 sts	88 sts	96 sts

KNITTING THE LOWER HAT

Next Rounds Work even in Stockinette Stitch until piece measures about 2½" (6.5 cm) from cast-on edge.			
Next 4 Rounds Join CC and work Rounds 1–4 of Waves and Tassels Chart, taking care to carry the unused strand of yarn loosely across the back of the work to prevent puckering.			
Next Round Cut CB; the remainder of hat is worked entirely using CC. Knit 1 round, decreasing	2 sts	4 sts	6 sts
You now have	78 sts	84 sts	90 sts

KNITTING THE CROWN

Note Change to double-pointed needles when there are too few stitches to fit comfortably around the circular needle.			
Round 1			
Small only: *K11, K2tog; repeat from * to end.			
Medium only: *K12, K2tog; repeat from * to end.			
Large only: *K13, K2tog; repeat from * to end.			
You now have	72 sts	78 sts	84 sts
Round 2 Knit.			
Round 3			
Small only: *K10, K2tog; repeat from * to end.			
Medium only: *K11, K2tog; repeat from * to end.			
Large only: *K12, K2tog; repeat from * to end.			
You now have	66 sts	72 sts	78 sts
Round 4 Knit.			

KNITTING THE CROWN (CONT'D)	SMALL	MEDIUM	LARGE
Round 5			
Small only: *K9, K2tog; repeat from * to end.			
Medium only: *K10, K2tog; repeat from * to end.			
Large only: *K11, K2tog; repeat from * to end.			
You now have	60 sts	66 sts	72 sts
Round 6 Knit.			
Round 7			
Small only: *K8, K2tog; repeat from * to end.			
Medium only: *K9, K2tog; repeat from * to end.			
Large only: *K10, K2tog; repeat from * to end.			
You now have	54 sts	60 sts	66 sts
Round 8 Knit.			
Round 9			
Small only: *K7, K2tog; repeat from * to end.			
Medium only: *K8, K2tog; repeat from * to end.			
Large only: *K9, K2tog; repeat from * to end.			
You now have	48 sts	54 sts	60 sts
Round 10 Knit.			
Next Rounds Continue in this manner, working a plain Stockinette Stitch round between each decrease round, and working 1 stitch less before the K2tog in each decrease round, until you have completed a round of *K1, K2tog; repeat from * to end: 12 stitches remain for all sizes.			
Next Round *K2tog; repeat from * to end. *You now have*	6 sts	6 sts	6 sts
Cut yarn leaving a 10" (25.5 cm) tail. Thread tail on tapestry needle and run through all stitches like a drawstring. Pull tail firmly to close top of hat, and weave in tail on wrong side.			

FINISHING

Weave in ends.

EMBROIDERY

Using a double strand of CD, embroider lines of running stitch (see page 196) along the first and last rounds of K2, P2 rib as shown, working running stitch over one knit stitch, then under the next knit stitch, and so on.

Using a single strand of CA, work chain stitch embroidery (see page 197) along the line of the color change from CB to CA of the charted section as shown, working a continuous, undulating line to smooth the color transition.

Using a double strand of CA, work a French Knot (see page 197) in each semi-circular section above and below the chain stitch line as shown, centering the French knots in each section and about 1" (2.5 cm) from chain stitching.

Using a double strand of CE, work a French knot about 1" (2.5 cm) above the "peak" of each chain stitch curve as shown.

TASSELS

Make one tassel (see page 199) each in CB, CD, and CE, making tassels about 4" or 5" (10 cm or 12.5 cm) tall: three tassels total. Tie each tassel's "head" with a 20" (51 cm) double strand of yarn made from two different colors. Braid the strands from the tassel heads for 2" to 6" (5 cm to 15 cm), making braids three different lengths. Secure the end of each braid with an overhand knot. Tie tassels to center top of hat. Weave in ends of braids on wrong side of hat.

Running stitch along color breaks; French knots above and below the chain stitch undulating line.

WAVES AND TASSELS CHART

■ CB ZINNIA PINK

■ CC BLUE THYME

Cozy
SOCKS

boot
toppers

i designed this project so that you'll have a fun, useful project at the same time you're knitting up a gauge swatch in the round. After knitting one boot topper, block it and measure the Fair Isle section to determine the gauge you got. The gauge should be as close as possible to the gauge in the next project you're going to make. It's especially useful when you're about to knit socks or mittens.

stitches

K2, P2 RIB
Work all rounds as *K2, P2; repeat from * to end of round.

STOCKINETTE STITCH
Knit all stitches every round.

REVERSE STOCKINETTE RIDGE
Round 1 Knit.
Rounds 2 and 3 Purl.

YARN

Nashua Handknits Julia, 50% wool/ 25% mohair/25% alpaca, 93 yd (85 m)/ 50 g. Yarn band gauge: 5 stitches and 6 rows = 1" (2.5 cm) in Stockinette Stitch on US 7 (4.5 mm) needles.

Diamond Boot Topper (above right):
CA = 8118 Espresso, 1 skein
CB = 0178 Harvest Spice, 1 skein
CC = 3961 Ladies Mantle, 1 skein
CD = 4936 Blue Thyme, 1 skein

Checked Boot Topper (above left):
CA = 4345 Coleus, 1 skein
CB = 1220 Tarnished Brass, 1 skein
CC = 4936 Blue Thyme, 1 skein
CD = 2230 Rock Henna, 1 skein

FINISHED SIZE

10½" to 11½" (26.5 to 29 cm) circumference at colorwork end, and about 8" to 9" (20.5 to 23 cm) tall

GAUGE

No gauge is given, because this project is intended to serve as a gauge swatch for working in the round.

NEEDLES

Set of four US 5, 6, 7, or 8 (3.75, 4, 4.5, or 5 mm) double-pointed needles *or size specified in the pattern for which you are trying to match gauge*

NOTIONS

Tapestry needle
Stitch marker

ABBREVIATIONS

inc = increase

boot toppers

KNITTING THE RIBBED CUFF

Set Up   Using CA, cast on 44 stitches.

Divide stitches as evenly as possible on three needles, place marker, and join for working in the round, being careful not to twist stitches. Work in K2, P2 Rib for 4" (10 cm).

Next 2 Rounds   Purl all stitches. This creates a fold line so that when you wear the boot toppers with the ribbing tucked inside the boot the colorwork section can be folded down over the outside of the boot.

Next Round   *P7, inc 1 using the backward loop cast-on method (see page 200); repeat from * to last 2 stitches, P2.
You now have 50 stitches.

KNITTING THE COLORWORK TOP

Work according to the instructions for either the Diamond Boot Topper or Checked Boot Topper below.

Diamond Boot Topper

Rounds 1–3   Change to CD. Work 1 Reverse Stockinette Ridge.

Rounds 4–18   Work in pattern from Diamond Boot Topper Chart opposite, using CA and CB until Round 15 has been completed.

Rounds 19–21   Change to CC. Work 1 Reverse Stockinette Ridge.

Rounds 22–24   Change to CD. Work 1 Reverse Stockinette Ridge.

Change to CA, and bind off all stitches firmly and neatly, allowing the bound-off edge to stretch enough to fit over boots.

Using a single strand of CC, work duplicate stitch embroidery (see page 194) around the outer edge of each large diamond motif as shown on embroidery chart. Weave in ends. Steam or block to even out colorwork.

OR

Checked Boot Topper

Rounds 1–3   In CA work 1 Reverse Stockinette Ridge.

Rounds 4–12   Work in pattern from Checked Boot Topper Chart opposite, using CB, CC, and CD.

Rounds 13–18   Repeat Rounds 4–9 once more.

Next 3 Rounds   Change to CA. Work 1 Reverse Stockinette Ridge.

Using CA, bind off all stitches firmly and neatly, allowing the bound-off edge to stretch enough to fit over boots.

Weave in ends. Steam or block to even out colorwork.

DIAMOND BOOT TOPPER CHARTS

KNITTING YARN COLORS

■ CA ESPRESSO

■ CB HARVEST SPICE

KNITTING

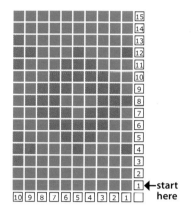

EMBROIDERY YARN COLOR

■ CC LADIES MANTLE

EMBROIDERY

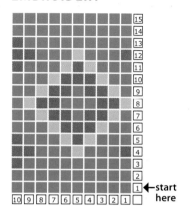

CHECKED BOOT TOPPER CHART

■ CB TARNISHED BRASS

■ CC BLUE THYME

■ CD ROCK HENNA

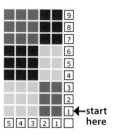

be happy, be colorful socks

Socks needn't be one color nor match! In fact, if they're multi-colored, it makes the knitting much more fun and less boring. And why cover them up with a pair of pants? Pull on some wacky tights, hike up a pair of colorful socks, and grab some clogs to create your own eccentric style. The combination of colors is, of course, endless. First time sock knitter? These are for you!

Plan of action: The socks are knitted from the top down to the toe on double-pointed needles. First you use stockinette stitch for a decorative rolled edge, then ribbing for the rest of the leg. The heel is knitted back and forth in rows and then you pick up stitches for the gusset and resume working in rounds. Decreases shape first the gusset and then finally the toe. You close the toe by grafting the final stitches together (see page 202).

stitches

K2, P2 RIB
Work all rounds as *K2, P2; repeat from * to end of round.

STOCKINETTE STITCH
Knit all stitches every round.

YARN

Nashua Handknits Julia, 50% wool/25% mohair/25% alpaca, 93 yd (85 m)/1¾ oz (50 g). Yarn band gauge: 5 stitches and 6 rows = 1" (2.5 cm) in Stockinette Stitch on US 7 (4.5 mm) needles.

5084 Zinnia Pink, 1 skein for all sizes

5185 Spring Green, 1 skein for Woman's small and medium; 2 skeins for Man's medium

2250 French Pumpkin, 1 skein for all sizes

5178 Lupine, 1 skein for Woman's small and medium; 2 skeins for Man's medium

SIZES AND FINISHED FOOT CIRCUMFERENCES

Woman's small, 7" (18 cm); Woman's medium, 8" (20.5 cm); Man's medium, 9" (23 cm)

Model shown in woman's medium.

GAUGE

20 stitches and 26 rounds = 4" (10 cm) in Stockinette Stitch worked in the round using larger needle.

NEEDLES

Set of four US 7 (4.5 mm) double-pointed needles *or size you need to obtain the correct gauge*

Set of four US 6 (4 mm) double-pointed needles

NOTIONS

Tapestry needle

Stitch marker

Stitch holder (optional)

Matching sewing thread (optional, for reinforcing heels)

ABBREVIATIONS

K2tog = knit 2 stitches together

P2tog = purl 2 stitches together

KNITTING THE LEG	WOMAN'S SMALL	WOMAN'S MEDIUM	MAN'S MEDIUM
Note Be sure to cast on loosely so the top of the sock will fit over your ankle.			
Set Up Using CA and smaller needles, loosely cast on	36 sts	40 sts	44 sts
Divide stitches on three needles as follows (each number is how many stitches to place on one double-pointed needle):	12, 12, 12 sts	13, 13, 14 sts	14, 15, 15 sts
Place marker and join for working in the round, being careful not to twist stitches.			
Next 6 Rounds Work in Stockinette Stitch. The fabric will curl to create a decorative rolled edge at top of sock.			
Next Round Change to CB and knit 1 round.			
Next Rounds Work in K2, P2 Rib until ribbing measures 3" (7.5 cm) from first round of CB.			
Next Rounds Change to larger needles. Continue in K2, P2 Rib until ribbing measures from first round of CB	6½" (16.5 cm)	7" (18 cm)	8" (20.5 cm)
Next 3 Rounds Change to CC. Knit 1 round, then purl 2 rounds.			
KNITTING THE HEEL			
Change to CA.			
Set Up Knit onto a single needle for heel the first	18 sts	20 sts	22 sts
Divide the remaining stitches evenly on two needles for instep, or place them on a stitch holder while working the heel.			

a fun mismatch

Try this: Make the first sock according to the color assignments for Sock 1, then make the second sock using the colors given for Sock 2 to create a fun pair of mismatched socks.

Sock 1:
CA = 5084 Zinnia Pink
CB = 5185 Spring Green
CC = 2250 French Pumpkin
CD = 5178 Lupine

Sock 2:
CA = 2250 French Pumpkin
CB = 5178 Lupine
CC = 5084 Zinnia Pink
CD = 5185 Spring Green

KNITTING THE HEEL (CONT'D)	WOMAN'S SMALL	WOMAN'S MEDIUM	MAN'S MEDIUM
The heel flap is worked back and forth in rows on the stitches of the heel needle only. Turn the needle with the heel stitches so the wrong side of the work is facing you, and continue as follows:			

The heel flap is worked back and forth in rows on the stitches of the heel needle only. Turn the needle with the heel stitches so the wrong side of the work is facing you, and continue as follows:

Row 1 (wrong side) K1, purl to last stitch, K1.

Row 2 (right side) K1, *K1, slip 1 stitch as if to purl with yarn in back; repeat from * to last stitch, K1.

Repeat Rows 1 and 2, ending with a right side row, until heel flap measures

	WOMAN'S SMALL	WOMAN'S MEDIUM	MAN'S MEDIUM
Repeat Rows 1 and 2... until heel flap measures	2" (5 cm)	2" (5 cm)	2¼" (5.5 cm)

Work the heel turning using short rows as follows:

Row 1 (wrong side)

Purl

	WOMAN'S SMALL	WOMAN'S MEDIUM	MAN'S MEDIUM
Purl	11 sts	12 sts	13 sts

P2tog, P1, turn.

Row 2 (right side) Slip the first stitch as if to purl with yarn in back, K5, slip 1 stitch as if to knit with yarn in back, K1, pass slipped stitch over, K1, turn.

Row 3 Slip the first stitch as if to purl with yarn in front, P6, P2tog, P1, turn.

Row 4 Slip the first stitch as if to purl with yarn in back, K7, slip 1 stitch as if to knit with yarn in back, K1, pass slipped stitch over, K1, turn.

Row 5 Slip the first stitch as if to purl with yarn in front, P8, P2tog, P1, turn.

Row 6 Slip the first stitch as if to purl with yarn in back, K9, slip 1 stitch as if to knit with yarn in back, K1, pass slipped stitch over, K1.

For Woman's small only: You now have 12 heel stitches; go to Knitting the Gusset.

For Woman's medium only:

Row 7 (wrong side) Slip the first stitch as if to purl with yarn in front, P10, P2tog, turn.

Row 8 Slip the first stitch as if to purl with yarn in back, K10, slip 1 stitch as if to knit with yarn in back, K1, pass slipped stitch over.

You now have 12 heel stitches; go to Knitting the Gusset.

For Man's medium only:

Row 7 (wrong side) Slip the first stitch as if to purl with yarn in front, P10, P2tog, P1, turn.

KNITTING THE HEEL (CONT'D)	WOMAN'S SMALL	WOMAN'S MEDIUM	MAN'S MEDIUM
Row 8 Slip the first stitch as if to purl with yarn in back, K10, slip 1 stitch as if to knit with yarn in back, K1, pass slipped stitch over, K1, turn.			
Row 9 Slip the first stitch as if to purl with yarn in front, P11, P2tog, turn.			
Row 10 Slip the first stitch as if to purl with yarn in back, K10, slip 1 stitch as if to knit with yarn in back, K1, pass slipped stitch over.			

You now have 12 heel stitches; go to Knitting the Gusset.

KNITTING THE GUSSET

Place all instep stitches on a single needle. Change to CD.

	WOMAN'S SMALL	WOMAN'S MEDIUM	MAN'S MEDIUM
Set Up With right side facing and using the needle holding the heel stitches, pick up and knit along selvedge of heel flap	12 sts	12 sts	13 sts
With another needle, knit across from instep	18 sts	20 sts	22 sts
With a third needle, pick up and knit from other selvedge of heel flap	12 sts	12 sts	13 sts

Knit the first 6 stitches from heel needle onto the end of the third needle.

You now have	WOMAN'S SMALL	WOMAN'S MEDIUM	MAN'S MEDIUM
On Needle 1	18 sts	18 sts	19 sts
On Needle 2	18 sts	20 sts	22 sts
On Needle 3	18 sts	18 sts	19 sts
Total stitches:	54 sts	56 sts	60 sts

Place marker to indicate beginning of round at center back heel.

Gusset Round 1

Needle 1: Knit to last 3 stitches K2tog, K1.

Needle 2: Knit

Needle 3: K1, slip 1 stitch as if to knit with yarn in back, K1, pass slipped stitch over, knit to end.

2 stitches decreased, 1 stitch each from Needles 1 and 3.

Gusset Round 2 Knit.

	WOMAN'S SMALL	WOMAN'S MEDIUM	MAN'S MEDIUM
Repeat the last 2 rounds	8 more times	7 more times	7 more times
You now have	36 sts	40 sts	44 sts

KNITTING THE FOOT

	WOMAN'S SMALL	WOMAN'S MEDIUM	MAN'S MEDIUM
Work even in Stockinette Stitch until foot measures from center back heel	6½" (16.5 cm)	7¾" (19.5 cm)	8½" (21.5 cm)
Or about this much less than desired total foot length:	1¾" (4.5 cm)	2¼" (5.5 cm)	2¼" (5.5 cm)

KNITTING THE TOE	WOMAN'S SMALL	WOMAN'S MEDIUM	MAN'S MEDIUM
Change to CC.			

Toe Round 1

Needle 1: Knit to last 3 stitches K2tog, K1

Needle 2: K1, slip 1 stitch as if to knit with yarn in back, K1, pass slipped stitch over, knit to last 3 stitches, K2tog, K1

Needle 3: K1, slip 1 stitch as if to knit with yarn in back, K1, pass slipped stitch over, knit to end.

4 stitches decreased, 1 stitch each from Needles 1 and 3, and 2 stitches from Needle 2.

Toe Round 2 Knit.

	WOMAN'S SMALL	WOMAN'S MEDIUM	MAN'S MEDIUM
Repeat the last 2 rounds	5 more times	6 more times	6 more times
You now have	12 sts	12 sts	16 sts
Place stitches from Needles 1 and 3 on one needle for bottom of toe.			
You now have on 2 needles	6 stitches each	6 stitches each	8 stitches each

FINISHING

Graft toe stitches together to close toe (see page 202).

Weave in ends.

stronger heels

The slipstitch pattern I use for all the socks' heel flaps is naturally thicker and more hard-wearing than plain stockinette, but for an even more durable heel, knit a strand of matching sewing thread held together with the main yarn in the heel section, for reinforcement.

wild and woolly socks

Over the years, I've had many discussions with the indomitable Jackie Katzenstein, owner of a yarn store in Lexington, Massachusetts, about her color likes and dislikes. Jackie has dark black hair and loves reds, blues, blacks, and whites, in combination or alone. I, on the other hand, have always loved autumn-feeling colors — like those in these socks. I've tended to make garments in colors I like, naturally. Although we've debated for years, we love each other, as friends do, especially knitting friends with opinions! Grab four of your own favorite colors, and create your "wild and woolly" pair. Add a few French knots and some cross-stitch and your socks will definitely be uniquely you.

Plan of action: The socks are knitted from the top down to the toe on double-pointed needles. First the leg is knitted in the round with K2, P2 ribbing, then the heel is knitted back and forth in rows, and then you pick up stitches for the gusset and resume working in rounds. Decreases shape first the gusset and then finally the toe. You close the toe by grafting the final stitches together (see page 202).

stitches

> **K2, P2 RIB**
> Work all rounds as *K2, P2; repeat from * to end of round.
>
> **STOCKINETTE STITCH**
> Knit all stitches every round.
>
> **STRIPE PATTERN**
> **Rounds 1–4** Knit 4 rounds with CA.
> **Rounds 5–8** Knit 4 rounds with CD.
> Repeat these 8 rounds for stripe pattern.

YARN

Nashua Handknits Julia, 50% wool/25% mohair/25% alpaca, 93 yd (85 m)/1¾ oz (50 g). Yarn band gauge: 5 stitches and 6 rows = 1" (2.5 cm) in Stockinette Stitch on US 7 (4.5 mm) needles.

CA = 0178 Harvest Spice, 1 skein for all sizes
CB = 3961 Ladies Mantle, 1 skein for Woman's small and medium; 2 skeins for Man's medium
CC = 4330 Mushroom, 1 skein for all sizes
CD = 4936 Blue Thyme, 1 skein for all sizes

SIZES AND FINISHED FOOT CIRCUMFERENCES

Woman's small, 7" (18 cm); Woman's medium, 8" (20.5 cm); Man's medium, 9" (23 cm)

Model shown in woman's medium.

GAUGE

20 stitches and 26 rounds = 4" (10 cm) in Stockinette Stitch worked in the round using larger needle.

NEEDLES

Set of four US 7 (4.5 mm) double-pointed needles *or size you need to obtain the correct gauge*

Set of four US 6 (4 mm) double-pointed needles

NOTIONS

Tapestry needle

Stitch marker

Stitch holder (optional)

Matching sewing thread (optional for reinforcing heels; see Tip, page 77)

ABBREVIATIONS

K2tog = knit 2 stitches together
P2tog = purl 2 stitches together

KNITTING THE LEG	WOMAN'S SMALL	WOMAN'S MEDIUM	MAN'S MEDIUM
Cast on loosely so the top of the leg will fit over your ankle.			
Set Up Using CA and smaller needles, loosely cast on	36 sts	40 sts	44 sts
Divide stitches among three needles as follows (each number is how many stitches to place on one double-pointed needle):	12, 12, 12 sts	13, 13, 14 sts	14, 15, 15 sts
Place marker and join for working in the round, being careful not to twist stitches.			
Next 4 Rounds Work in K2, P2 Rib.			
Next Rounds Change to CB. Continue in K2, P2 Rib until ribbing measures 3" (7.5 cm) from first round of CB.			
Next Rounds Change to larger needles. Continue in K2, P2 Rib until ribbing measures from first round of CB	6½" (16.5 cm)	7" (18 cm)	8" (20.5 cm)
KNITTING THE HEEL			
Set Up Change to CC. Knit onto a single needle for heel the first	18 sts	20 sts	22 sts
Divide the remaining stitches evenly on two needles for instep, or place them on a stitch holder while working the heel.			
The heel flap is worked back and forth in rows on the stitches of the heel needle only. Turn the needle with the heel stitches so the wrong side of the work is facing you, and continue as follows:			
Row 1 (wrong side) K1, purl to last stitch, K1.			
Row 2 (right side) K1, *K1, slip 1 stitch as if to purl with yarn in back; repeat from * to last stitch, K1.			
Repeat Rows 1 and 2, ending with a right side row, until heel flap measures	2" (5 cm)	2" (5 cm)	2¼" (5.5 cm)
Work the heel turning using short rows as follows:			
Row 1 (wrong side) Purl P2tog, P1, turn.	11 sts	12 sts	13 sts
Row 2 (right side) Slip the first stitch as if to purl with yarn in back, K5, slip 1 stitch as if to knit with yarn in back, K1, pass slipped stitch over, K1, turn.			
Row 3 Slip the first stitch as if to purl with yarn in front, P6, P2tog, P1, turn.			
Row 4 Slip the first stitch as if to purl with yarn in back, K7, slip 1 stitch as if to knit with yarn in back, K1, pass slipped stitch over, K1, turn.			
Row 5 Slip the first stitch as if to purl with yarn in front, P8, P2tog, P1, turn.			

KNITTING THE HEEL (CONT'D)	WOMAN'S SMALL	WOMAN'S MEDIUM	MAN'S MEDIUM

Row 6 Slip the first stitch as if to purl with yarn in back, K9, slip 1 stitch as if to knit with yarn in back, K1, pass slipped stitch over, K1.

Woman's small only: *You now have* 12 heel stitches; go to Knitting the Gusset.

For Woman's medium only:

Row 7 (wrong side) Slip the first stitch as if to purl with yarn in front, P10, P2tog, turn.

Row 8 Slip the first stitch as if to purl with yarn in back, K10, slip 1 stitch as if to knit with yarn in back, K1, pass slipped stitch over. *You now have* 12 heel stitches; go to Knitting the Gusset.

For Man's medium only:

Row 7 (wrong side) Slip the first stitch as if to purl with yarn in front, P10, P2tog, P1, turn.

Row 8 Slip the first stitch as if to purl with yarn in back, K10, slip 1 stitch as if to knit with yarn in back, K1, pass slipped stitch over, K1, turn.

Row 9 Slip the first stitch as if to purl with yarn in front, P11, P2tog, turn.

Row 10 Slip the first stitch as if to purl with yarn in back, K10, slip 1 stitch as if to knit with yarn in back, K1, pass slipped stitch over. *You now have* 12 heel stitches; go to Knitting the Gusset.

KNITTING THE GUSSET

	WOMAN'S SMALL	WOMAN'S MEDIUM	MAN'S MEDIUM
Set Up Place all instep stitches on a single needle. Change to CA. With right side facing and using the needle holding the heel stitches, pick up and knit along selvedge of heel flap	12 sts	12 sts	13 sts
With another needle, knit across from instep	18 sts	20 sts	22 sts
With a third needle, pick up and knit from other selvedge of heel flap	12 sts	12 sts	13 sts
Knit the first 6 stitches from heel needle onto the end of the third needle.			
You now have			
On Needle 1:	18 sts	18 sts	19 sts
On Needle 2:	18 sts	20 sts	22 sts
On Needle 3:	18 sts	18 sts	19 sts
Total stitches:	54 sts	56 sts	60 sts

KNITTING THE GUSSET (CONT'D)	WOMAN'S SMALL	WOMAN'S MEDIUM	MAN'S MEDIUM
The round just completed counts as Round 1 of Stripe Pattern. Place marker to indicate beginning of round at center back heel. Continue in Stripe Pattern (work 3 more rounds of CA to complete first stripe, then alternate 4 rounds each of CD and CA) while shaping gusset as follows:			

Gusset Round 1

> Needle 1: Knit to last 3 stitches K2tog, K1

> Needle 2: Knit.

> Needle 3: K1, slip 1 stitch as if to knit with yarn in back, K1, pass slipped stitch over, knit to end.

2 stitches decreased, 1 stitch each from Needles 1 and 3.

Gusset Round 2   Knit.

	WOMAN'S SMALL	WOMAN'S MEDIUM	MAN'S MEDIUM
Repeat the last 2 rounds	8 more times	7 more times	7 more times
You now have	36 sts	40 sts	44 sts

KNITTING THE FOOT

	WOMAN'S SMALL	WOMAN'S MEDIUM	MAN'S MEDIUM
Continue in Stripe Pattern until foot measures from center back heel about	6½" (16.5 cm)	7¾" (19.5 cm)	8½" (21.5 cm)
Or about this much less than desired total foot length:	1¾" (4.5 cm)	2¼" (5.5 cm)	2¼" (5.5 cm)
End having just finished a complete 4-round stripe.			

KNITTING THE TOE

Change to CB.

Toe Round 1

> Needle 1: Knit to last 3 stitches K2tog, K1

> Needle 2: K1, slip 1 stitch as if to knit with yarn in back, K1, pass slipped stitch over, knit to last 3 stitches, K2tog, K1.

> Needle 3: K1, slip 1 stitch as if to knit with yarn in back, K1, pass slipped stitch over, knit to end.

4 stitches decreased, 1 stitch each from Needles 1 and 3, and 2 stitches from Needle 2.

Toe Round 2   Knit.

	WOMAN'S SMALL	WOMAN'S MEDIUM	MAN'S MEDIUM
Repeat the last 2 rounds	5 more times	6 more times	6 more times
You now have	12 sts	12 sts	16 sts
Place stitches from Needles 1 and 3 on one needle for bottom of toe.			
You now have on 2 needles	6 stitches each	6 stitches each	8 stitches each

FINISHING

Graft toe stitches together to close toe (see page 202). Weave in ends.

EMBROIDERY

Note Carry the embroidery yarns loosely on the wrong side of the sock between each pair of stitches so the embroidered sections have the same amount of stretch as the rest of the sock.

Using a single strand of CC, embroider cross stitches around top of leg, working one cross stitch in each K2 column of the CA rib section as shown.

Using a double strand of CD, embroider French knots (see page 197) with about 2 stitches between each pair of knots around the top of the foot where the ribbing meets the stripe pattern as shown.

Cross stitches at top of ribbing.

French knots at base of ribbing.

striping wisdom

For the foot stripes, do not cut the yarn at each color change. Instead, carry the yarn not in use up the inside of the sock until it is needed again, then begin working with it once more. Try to carry the yarn loosely enough that it does not cause the sock fabric to pucker, but not so loosely that you snag the strands when you put on the sock.

atlantic and pacific socks

time spent on both coasts of the United States inspired these socks. The Maine Coast colorway evokes memories of the shimmering blue-green of the ocean. The Pacific Sunset colorway was inspired by Oregon's colorful sunsets.

Plan of action: The socks are knitted from the top down on double-pointed needles. Work either a bobbled edge or a decorative rolled edge, then knit the rest of the leg in K2, P2 ribbing. The heel is knitted back and forth in rows and then you pick up stitches for the gusset and resume working in rounds. Decreases shape first the gusset and then finally the toe. You close the toe by grafting the final stitches together.

YARN

Nashua Handknits Julia, 50% wool/25% mohair/25% alpaca, 93 yd (85 m)/1¾ oz (50 g). Yarn band gauge: 5 stitches and 6 rows = 1" (2.5 cm) in Stockinette Stitch on US 7 (4.5 mm) needles.

Pacific Sunset Colorway:
CA = 3961 Ladies Mantle, 1 skein for all sizes
CB = 2083 Magenta, 1 skein for all sizes
CC = 2250 French Pumpkin, 1 skein for all sizes

CD = 8126 Dried Lavender, 1 skein for Woman's small and medium; 2 skeins for Man's medium

Maine Coast Colorway:
CA = 5178 Lupine, 1 skein for all sizes
CB = 6396 Deep Blue Sea, 1 skein for all sizes
CC = 3961 Ladies Mantle, 1 skein for all sizes
CD = 4936 Blue Thyme, 1 skein for Woman's small and medium; 2 skeins for Man's medium

SIZES AND FINISHED FOOT CIRCUMFERENCES

Woman's small, 7" (18 cm); Woman's medium, 8" (20.5 cm); Man's medium, 9" (23 cm)

Models shown in woman's medium in Pacific Sunset with bobble edging, and man's medium in Maine Coast with rolled edge.

GAUGE

20 stitches and 26 rounds = 4" (10 cm) in Stockinette Stitch worked in the round using larger needle.

NEEDLES

Set of four US 7 (4.5 mm) double-pointed needles *or size you need to obtain the correct gauge*

Set of four US 6 (4 mm) double-pointed needles (for woman's sizes only)

NOTIONS

Tapestry needle

Stitch marker

Stitch holder (optional)

Matching sewing thread (optional for reinforcing heels; see Tip, page 77)

ABBREVIATIONS

K2tog = knit 2 stitches together
P2tog = purl 2 stitches together

stitches

BOBBLE EDGING
*P3, (K1, P1, K1, P1) all in same stitch to increase 1 stitch to 4 stitches, turn work so wrong side is facing, K4 bobble stitches, turn work so right side is facing, P4 bobble stitches, pass second, third, and fourth stitches on right needle over first stitch to decrease bobble back to 1 st; repeat from * to end of round.

CORRUGATED RIB
Set Up Round *K2 with CC, K2 with CD; repeat from * to end.
All Other Rounds *K2 with CC, take CC to back of work, bring CD to front of work, P2 with CD, bring CD to back of work; repeat from * to end. Repeat the last round only for pattern; do not repeat the Set Up Round.

GARTER RIDGE
Round 1 Knit.
Round 2 Purl.

REVERSE STOCKINETTE RIDGE
Round 1 Knit.
Rounds 2 and 3 Purl.

STOCKINETTE STITCH
Knit all stitches every round.

KNITTING THE LEG	WOMAN'S SMALL	WOMAN'S MEDIUM	MAN'S MEDIUM
Note Cast on loosely so the top of the leg will fit over your ankle.			
Set Up Using CA and larger needles, loosely cast on	36 sts	40 sts	44 sts
Divide stitches among three needles as follows (each number is how many stitches to place on one double-pointed needle):	12, 12, 12 sts	13, 13, 14 sts	14, 15, 15 sts
Place marker and join for working in the round, being careful not to twist stitches. Work the edging of your choice as follows:			

Bobbled Edge

Next Round Work according to Bobbled Edging instructions.

Next 2 Rounds Work 1 Garter Ridge.

Rolled Edge

Next 6 Rounds Work in Stockinette Stitch. The fabric will curl to create a decorative rolled edge at top of sock.

For All Versions

	WOMAN'S SMALL	WOMAN'S MEDIUM	MAN'S MEDIUM
Next Rounds Change to CB and CC. Work in Corrugated Rib until piece measures 3" (7.5 cm) from beginning.			
For women's sizes only: Change to smaller needles.			
For all sizes: Continue in Corrugated Rib until sock measures from first round of Corrugated Rib	6½" (16.5 cm)	7" (18 cm)	8" (20.5 cm)
Next 4 Rounds Change to CA.			
For women's sizes only: Change to larger needles.			
For all sizes: Work 2 Garter Ridges.			

KNITTING THE HEEL	WOMAN'S SMALL	WOMAN'S MEDIUM	MAN'S MEDIUM
Set Up Change to CB. Knit onto a single needle for heel the first	18 sts	20 sts	22 sts
Divide the remaining stitches evenly on two needles for instep, or place them on a stitch holder while working the heel.			
The heel flap is worked back and forth in rows on the stitches of the heel needle only. If desired, reinforce heel using matching sewing thread (see page 77). Turn the needle with the heel stitches so the wrong side of the work is facing you, and continue as follows:			
Row 1 (wrong side) K1, purl to last stitch, K1.			
Row 2 (right side) K1, *K1, slip 1 stitch as if to purl with yarn in back; repeat from * to last stitch, K1.			
Repeat Rows 1 and 2, ending with a right side row, until heel flap measures	2" (5 cm)	2" (5 cm)	2¼" (5.5 cm)

KNITTING THE HEEL (CONT'D)	WOMAN'S SMALL	WOMAN'S MEDIUM	MAN'S MEDIUM
Work the heel turning using short rows as follows:			

Row 1 (wrong side)

	WOMAN'S SMALL	WOMAN'S MEDIUM	MAN'S MEDIUM
Purl	11 sts	12 sts	13 sts

P2tog, P1, turn.

Row 2 (right side) Slip the first stitch as if to purl with yarn in back, K5, slip 1 stitch as if to knit with yarn in back, K1, pass slipped stitch over, K1, turn.

Row 3 Slip the first stitch as if to purl with yarn in front, P6, P2tog, P1, turn.

Row 4 Slip the first stitch as if to purl with yarn in back, K7, slip 1 stitch as if to knit with yarn in back, K1, pass slipped stitch over, K1, turn.

Row 5 Slip the first stitch as if to purl with yarn in front, P8, P2tog, P1, turn.

Row 6 Slip the first stitch as if to purl with yarn in back, K9, slip 1 stitch as if to knit with yarn in back, K1, pass slipped stitch over, K1.

For Woman's small only: You now have 12 heel stitches; go to Knitting the Gusset.

For Woman's medium only:

Row 7 (wrong side) Slip the first stitch as if to purl with yarn in front, P10, P2tog, turn.

Row 8 Slip the first stitch as if to purl with yarn in back, K10, slip 1 stitch as if to knit with yarn in back, K1, pass slipped stitch over.

You now have 12 heel stitches; go to Knitting the Gusset.

For Man's medium only:

Row 7 (wrong side) Slip the first stitch as if to purl with yarn in front, P10, P2tog, P1, turn.

Row 8 Slip the first stitch as if to purl with yarn in back, K10, slip 1 stitch as if to knit with yarn in back, K1, pass slipped stitch over, K1, turn.

Row 9 Slip the first stitch as if to purl with yarn in front, P11, P2tog, turn.

Row 10 Slip the first stitch as if to purl with yarn in back, K10, slip 1 stitch as if to knit with yarn in back, K1, pass slipped stitch over.

You now have 12 heel stitches; go to Knitting the Gusset.

KNITTING THE GUSSET	WOMAN'S SMALL	WOMAN'S MEDIUM	MAN'S MEDIUM
Set Up Place all instep stitches on a single needle. Change to CD. With right side facing and using the needle holding the heel stitches, pick up and knit along selvedge of heel flap	12 sts	12 sts	13 sts
With another needle, knit across from instep	18 sts	20 sts	22 sts
With a third needle, pick up and knit from other selvedge of heel flap	12 sts	12 sts	13 sts
Knit the first 6 stitches from heel needle onto the end of the third needle. *You now have*			
On Needle 1:	18 sts	18 sts	19 sts
On Needle 2:	18 sts	20 sts	22 sts
On Needle 3:	18 sts	18 sts	19 sts
Total stitches:	54 sts	56 sts	60 sts

Place marker to indicate beginning of round at center back heel. Continue in Stockinette Stitch while shaping gusset as follows:

Gusset Round 1

Needle 1: Knit to last 3 stitches, K2tog, K1

Needle 2: Knit.

Needle 3: K1, slip 1 stitch as if to knit with yarn in back, K1, pass slipped stitch over, knit to end: 2 stitches decreased, 1 stitch each from Needles 1 and 3.

Gusset Round 2 Knit.

	WOMAN'S SMALL	WOMAN'S MEDIUM	MAN'S MEDIUM
Repeat the last 2 rounds	8 more times	7 more times	7 more times
You now have	36 sts	40 sts	44 sts

KNITTING THE FOOT

	WOMAN'S SMALL	WOMAN'S MEDIUM	MAN'S MEDIUM
Continue in Stockinette Stitch until foot measures from center back heel about	6½" (16.5 cm)	7¾" (19.5 cm)	8½" (21.5 cm)
Or about this much less than desired total foot length:	1¾" (4.5 cm)	2¼" (5.5 cm)	2¼" (5.5 cm)

KNITTING THE TOE

Toe Round 1 Change to CC.

Needle 1: Knit to last 3 stitches, K2tog, K1.

Needle 2: K1, slip 1 stitch as if to knit with yarn in back, K1, pass slipped stitch over, knit to last 3 stitches, K2tog, K1.

Needle 3: K1, slip 1 stitch as if to knit with yarn in back, K1, pass slipped stitch over, knit to end.

4 stitches decreased, 1 stitch each from Needles 1 and 3, and 2 stitches from Needle 2.

Toe Round 2 Knit.

KNITTING THE TOE (CONT'D)	WOMAN'S SMALL	WOMAN'S MEDIUM	MAN'S MEDIUM
Repeat the last 2 rounds	5 more times	6 more times	6 more times
You now have	12 sts	12 sts	16 sts
Place stitches from Needles 1 and 3 on one needle for bottom of toe. *You now have* on 2 needles	6 stitches each	6 stitches each	8 stitches each
Graft toe stitches together to close toe (see page 202).			

FINISHING

Weave in ends.

Even, Elegant Ribbing

To achieve even rib widths, with one rib consistently raised above the other throughout the ribbing, it's important to carry the yarns properly at the back of the work. One of the colors is always carried on top, while the other is always carried underneath the first when changing working yarns. See the illustration on page 192 for further explanation. Knitters who are able to work holding one color in the right hand and the other color in the left will find that this technique is easy to maintain — so long as they remember always to hold the same color in the proper hand when they pick up their work after not knitting for awhile!

autumn
leaves
socks

My very favorite time of year is autumn, with its crisp, clear air and changing foliage colors. I pile on wool sweaters, socks, and hats and spend entire days outside. I also know that autumn means it's time to knit, and knit I do. The colors of these socks are my favorites. If you're new to Fair Isle knitting, this is a good design to try, as the pattern repeats aren't too large. Just remember to keep your floats nice and loose, so you'll be able to easily pull the sock over your foot.

Plan of action: The socks are knitted from the top to the toe on double-pointed needles. Start with a decorative rolled edge in stockinette stitch and then knit the top of the leg in K2, P2 (corrugated) ribbing. Sections of diamond pattern, triangles, and checks (worked from charts) are set off by Reverse Stockinette Ridges. (See pages 191 and 195 for instructions on working from a chart.) The heel is knitted back and forth in rows, and then pick up stitches for the gusset and resume working in rounds. Decreases shape first the gusset and then finally the toe. You close the toe by grafting the final stitches together (see page 202).

stitches

CORRUGATED RIB
Set Up Round *K2 with CB, K2 with CC; repeat from * to end.
All Other Rounds *K2 with CB, take CB to back of work, bring CC to front of work, P2 with CC, bring CC to back of work; repeat from * to end.
Repeat the last round only for pattern; do not repeat the Set Up Round.

REVERSE STOCKINETTE RIDGE
Round 1 Knit.
Rounds 2 and 3 Purl.

STOCKINETTE STITCH
Knit all stitches every round.

YARN
Nashua Handknits Julia, 50% wool/ 25% mohair/25% alpaca, 93 yd (85 m)/ 1¾ oz (50 g). Yarn band gauge: 5 stitches and 6 rows = 1" (2.5 cm) in Stockinette Stitch on US 7 (4.5 mm) needles.

CA = 5185 Spring Green, 1 skein for all sizes
CB = 2230 Rock Henna, 2 skeins for all sizes
CC = 2163 Golden Honey, 1 skein for all sizes
CD = 2250 French Pumpkin, 1 skein for all sizes

SIZES AND FINISHED FOOT CIRCUMFERENCES
Woman's small, 7" (18 cm); Woman's medium, 8" (20.5 cm); Man's medium, 9" (23 cm)

Model shown in woman's medium.

GAUGE
20 stitches and 24 rounds = 4" (10 cm) solid color Stockinette Stitch worked in the round using smaller needles.
20 stitches and 24 rounds = 4" (10 cm) in Stockinette Stitch Fair Isle patterns from charts worked in the round using larger needles.

NEEDLES
Set of four US 7 (4.5 mm) double-pointed needles *or size you need to obtain the correct gauge*

Set of four US 6 (4 mm) double-pointed needles *or size you need to obtain the correct gauge*

NOTIONS
Tapestry needle

Stitch marker

Stitch holder (optional)

Matching sewing thread (optional for reinforcing heels; see Tip, page 77)

ABBREVIATIONS
K2tog = knit 2 stitches together
P2tog = purl 2 stitches together

KNITTING THE LEG

	WOMAN'S SMALL	WOMAN'S MEDIUM	MAN'S MEDIUM
Note Cast on loosely so the top of the leg will fit over your ankle.			
Set Up Using CA and larger needles, loosely cast on	36 sts	40 sts	44 sts
Divide stitches on three needles as follows (each number is how many stitches to place on one double-pointed needle):	12, 12, 12 sts	13, 13, 14 sts	14, 15, 15 sts
Place marker and join for working in the round, being careful not to twist stitches.			
Next 6 Rounds Work in Stockinette Stitch. The fabric will curl to create a decorative rolled edge at top of sock.			
Next Rounds Change to CB and CC. Work in Corrugated Rib until piece measures from beginning of rib pattern	1¾" (4.5 cm)	2" (5 cm)	2¼" (5.5 cm)
Next 3 Rounds Change to CD and work 1 Reverse Stockinette Ridge.			
Next 7 Rounds Change to smaller needles and, using CA and CC as shown, work Rounds 1–7 of Diamond Chart.			
Next 3 Rounds Change to CB and work 1 Reverse Stockinette Ridge.			
Next 6 Rounds Using CA and CD as shown, work Rounds 1–6 of Triangle Chart.			
Next 3 Rounds Change to CC and work 1 Reverse Stockinette Ridge.			
Next Rounds Using CB and CC as shown, repeat Rounds 1–4 of Checks Chart until piece measures from beginning with upper edge rolled	6½" (16.5 cm)	7" (18 cm)	8" (20.5 cm)
End with Round 2 or 4 of Checks Chart.			
Next 3 Rounds Change to larger needles and CA and work 1 Reverse Stockinette Ridge.			

KNITTING THE HEEL

	WOMAN'S SMALL	WOMAN'S MEDIUM	MAN'S MEDIUM
Change to CC.			
Set Up Knit onto a single needle for heel the first	18 sts	20 sts	22 sts
Divide the remaining stitches evenly on two needles for instep, or place them on a stitch holder while working the heel.			

The heel flap is worked back and forth in rows on the stitches of the heel needle only. If desired, reinforce heel using matching sewing thread (see Tip on page 77). Turn the needle with the heel stitches so the wrong side of the work is facing you, and continue as follows:

Row 1 (wrong side)   K1, purl to last stitch, K1.

Row 2 (right side)   K1, *K1, slip 1 stitch as if to purl with yarn in back; repeat from * to last stitch, K1.

KNITTING THE HEEL (CONT'D)	WOMAN'S SMALL	WOMAN'S MEDIUM	MAN'S MEDIUM
Repeat Rows 1 and 2, ending with a right side row, until heel flap measures	2" (5 cm)	2" (5 cm)	2¼" (5.5 cm)

Work the heel turning using short rows as follows:

Row 1 (wrong side)

Purl	11 sts	12 sts	13 sts

P2tog, P1, turn.

Row 2 (right side) Slip the first stitch as if to purl with yarn in back, K5, slip 1 stitch as if to knit with yarn in back, K1, pass slipped stitch over, K1, turn.

Row 3 Slip the first stitch as if to purl with yarn in front, P6, P2tog, P1, turn.

Row 4 Slip the first stitch as if to purl with yarn in back, K7, slip 1 stitch as if to knit with yarn in back, K1, pass slipped stitch over, K1, turn.

Row 5 Slip the first stitch as if to purl with yarn in front, P8, P2tog, P1, turn.

Row 6 Slip the first stitch as if to purl with yarn in back, K9, slip 1 stitch as if to knit with yarn in back, K1, pass slipped stitch over, K1.

For Woman's small only: You now have 12 heel stitches; go to Knitting the Gusset.

For Woman's medium only:

Row 7 (wrong side) Slip the first stitch as if to purl with yarn in front, P10, P2tog, turn.

Row 8 Slip the first stitch as if to purl with yarn in back, K10, slip 1 stitch as if to knit with yarn in back, K1, pass slipped stitch over. *You now have* 12 heel stitches; go to Knitting the Gusset.

For Man's medium only:

Row 7 (wrong side) Slip the first stitch as if to purl with yarn in front, P10, P2tog, P1, turn.

Row 8 Slip the first stitch as if to purl with yarn in back, K10, slip 1 stitch as if to knit with yarn in back, K1, pass slipped stitch over, K1, turn.

Row 9 Slip the first stitch as if to purl with yarn in front, P11, P2tog, turn.

Row 10 Slip the first stitch as if to purl with yarn in back, K10, slip 1 stitch as if to knit with yarn in back, K1, pass slipped stitch over. *You now have* 12 heel stitches; go to Knitting the Gusset.

KNITTING THE GUSSET	WOMAN'S SMALL	WOMAN'S MEDIUM	MAN'S MEDIUM
Set Up Place all instep stitches on a single needle. Change to CB.			
With right side facing and using the needle holding the heel stitches, pick up and knit along selvedge of heel flap	12 sts	12 sts	13 sts
With another needle, knit across from instep	18 sts	20 sts	22 sts
With a third needle, pick up and knit from other selvedge of heel flap	12 sts	12 sts	13 sts
Knit the first 6 stitches from heel needle onto the end of the third needle.			
You now have			
On Needle 1:	18 sts	18 sts	19 sts
On Needle 2:	18 sts	20 sts	22 sts
On Needle 3:	18 sts	18 sts	19 sts
Total stitches:	54 sts	56 sts	60 sts

Place marker to indicate beginning of round at center back heel.
Continue in Stockinette Stitch while shaping gusset as follows:

Gusset Round 1

Needle 1: Knit to last 3 stitches K2tog, K1

Needle 2: Knit

Needle 3: K1, slip 1 stitch as if to knit with yarn in back, K1, pass slipped stitch over, knit to end.

2 stitches decreased, 1 stitch each from Needles 1 and 3.

Gusset Round 2 Knit.

	WOMAN'S SMALL	WOMAN'S MEDIUM	MAN'S MEDIUM
Repeat the last 2 rounds	8 more times	7 more times	7 more times
You now have	36 sts	40 sts	44 sts

KNITTING THE FOOT

	WOMAN'S SMALL	WOMAN'S MEDIUM	MAN'S MEDIUM
Continue in Stockinette Stitch until foot measures from center back heel about	6½" (16.5 cm)	7¾" (19.5 cm)	8½" (21.5 cm)
Or about this much less than desired total foot length:	1¾" (4.5 cm)	2¼" (5.5 cm)	2¼" (5.5 cm)

KNITTING THE TOE

Toe Round 1 Change to CD.

Needle 1: Knit to last 3 stitches K2tog, K1;

Needle 2: K1, slip 1 stitch as if to knit with yarn in back, K1, pass slipped stitch over, knit to last 3 stitches, K2tog, K1;

Needle 3: K1, slip 1 stitch as if to knit with yarn in back, K1, pass slipped stitch over, knit to end:

4 stitches decreased, 1 stitch each from Needles 1 and 3, and 2 stitches from Needle 2.

KNITTING THE TOE (CONT'D)	WOMAN'S SMALL	WOMAN'S MEDIUM	MAN'S MEDIUM
Toe Round 2 Knit.			
Repeat the last 2 rounds	5 more times	6 more times	6 more times
You now have	12 sts	12 sts	16 sts
Place stitches from Needles 1 and 3 on one needle for bottom of toe. *You now have* on 2 needles	6 stitches each	6 stitches each	8 stitches each
FINISHING			
Graft toe stitches together to close toe (see page 202).			
Weave in ends.			

AUTUMN LEAVES SOCKS CHARTS

- ▣ **CA SPRING GREEN**
- ▣ **CB ROCK HENNA**
- ▢ **CC GOLDEN HONEY**
- ▣ **CD FRENCH PUMPKIN**

CHECKS CHART

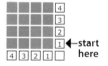

DIAMOND CHART

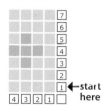

TRIANGLE CHART

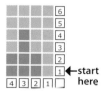

persian carpet socks

I have a large collection of Middle Eastern, flat-weave carpets called *kilims*. I often look to them for ideas to use in my knitwear designs. I love the way the rug-weavers combine colors and motifs to create their own distinct artwork for the floor. Here, I've borrowed their diamond design to knit a traditional two-color Fair Isle pattern, then added pink and teal duplicate stitching to create a very colorful pair of socks anyone would love.

Plan of action: The socks are knitted from the top down to the toe on double-pointed needles. Using the larger needles, you start with a decorative rolled edge in stockinette stitch and then knit the top of the leg in K2, P2 (corrugated) ribbing. A diamond pattern section is set off by Reverse Stockinette Ridges. (See pages 191 and 195 for instructions on following a chart.) The heel is knitted back and forth in rows and then you pick up stitches for the gusset and resume working in rounds. Decreases shape first the gusset and then finally the toe. You close the toe by grafting the final stitches together (see page 202).

stitches

CORRUGATED RIB
Set Up Round *K2 with CB, K2 with CC; repeat from * to end.
All Other Rounds *K2 with CB, take CB to back of work, bring CC to front of work, P2 with CC, bring CC to back of work; repeat from * to end.
Repeat the last round only for pattern; do not repeat the Set Up Round.

REVERSE STOCKINETTE RIDGE
Round 1 Knit.
Rounds 2 and 3 Purl.

STOCKINETTE STITCH
Knit all stitches every round.

SIZES AND FINISHED FOOT CIRCUMFERENCES

Woman's small, 7" (18 cm); Woman's medium, 8" (20.5 cm); Man's medium, 9" (23 cm)

Model shown in woman's medium.

GAUGE

20 stitches and 24 rounds = 4" (10 cm) solid color Stockinette Stitch worked in the round using larger needles.
20 stitches and 24 rounds = 4" (10 cm) in Stockinette Stitch Fair Isle patterns from charts worked in the round using larger needles.

NEEDLES

Set of four US 7 (4.5 mm) double-pointed needles *or size you need to obtain the correct gauge*

Set of four US 6 (4 mm) double-pointed needles *or size you need to obtain the correct gauge*

NOTIONS

Tapestry needle

Stitch marker

Stitch holder (optional)

Matching sewing thread (optional for reinforcing heels; see Tip, page 77)

ABBREVIATIONS

K2tog = knit 2 stitches together
P2tog = purl 2 stitches together

YARN

Nashua Handknits Julia, 50% wool/ 25% mohair/25% alpaca, 93 yd (85 m)/ 1¾ oz (50 g). Yarn band gauge: 5 stitches and 6 rows = 1" (2.5 cm) in Stockinette Stitch on US 7 (4.5 mm) needles.

CA = 4936 Blue Thyme, 1 skein for all sizes

CB = 8141 Pretty Pink, 1 skein for all sizes

CC = 6416 Midnight Blue, 1 skein for Woman's small and medium; 2 skeins for Man's medium

CD = 2250 French Pumpkin, 1 skein for all sizes

CE = 4345 Coleus, 1 skein for all sizes

KNITTING THE LEG	WOMAN'S SMALL	WOMAN'S MEDIUM	MAN'S MEDIUM
Note Cast on loosely so the top of the leg will fit over your ankle.			
Set Up Using CA and larger needles, loosely cast on	36 sts	40 sts	44 sts
Divide stitches on three needles as follows (each number is how many stitches to place on one double-pointed needle)	12, 12, 12 sts	13, 13, 14 sts	14, 15, 15 sts
Place marker and join for working in the round, being careful not to twist stitches.			
Next 6 Rounds Work in Stockinette Stitch. The fabric will curl to create a decorative rolled edge at top of sock.			
Next Rounds Change to CB and CC. Work in Corrugated Rib until piece measures from beginning of rib pattern	1¾" (4.5 cm)	2" (5 cm)	2¼" (5.5 cm
Next 3 Rounds Change to smaller needles and CA and work 1 Reverse Stockinette Ridge, increasing in first round	3 sts	2 sts	1 st
You now have	39 sts	42 sts	45 sts
Next 26 Rounds One pattern repeat from the Persian Carpet Socks Chart contains	13 sts	14 sts	15 sts
Using CD and CE as shown, repeat the Persian Carpet Socks Chart for your size 3 times for each round. Work in pattern from chart until Round 26 has been completed for all sizes.			
Next 3 Rounds Change to CA and work 1 Reverse Stockinette Ridge, decreasing in first round	3 sts	2 sts	1 st
You now have	36 sts	40 sts	44 sts
With upper edge rolled, piece measures from beginning about	6¾" (17 cm)	8" (20.5 cm)	8¼" (21 cm)
KNITTING THE HEEL			
Set Up Change to CD and the larger needles. Knit onto a single needle for heel the first	18 sts	20 sts	22 sts
Divide the remaining stitches evenly on two needles for instep, or place them on a stitch holder while working the heel.			
The heel flap is worked back and forth in rows on the stitches of the heel needle only. If desired, reinforce heel using matching sewing thread (see page 77). Turn the needle with the heel stitches so the wrong side of the work is facing you, and continue as follows:			
Row 1 (wrong side) K1, purl to last stitch, K1.			
Row 2 (right side) K1, *K1, slip 1 stitch as if to purl with yarn in back; repeat from * to last stitch, K1.			
Repeat Rows 1 and 2, ending with a right side row, until heel flap measures	2" (5 cm)	2" (5 cm)	2¼" (5.5 cm)

KNITTING THE HEEL (CONT'D)	WOMAN'S SMALL	WOMAN'S MEDIUM	MAN'S MEDIUM

Work the heel turning using short rows as follows:

Row 1 (wrong side)

| Purl | 11 sts | 12 sts | 13 sts |

P2tog, P1, turn.

Row 2 (right side) Slip the first stitch as if to purl with yarn in back, K5, slip 1 stitch as if to knit with yarn in back, K1, pass slipped stitch over, K1, turn.

Row 3 Slip the first stitch as if to purl with yarn in front, P6, P2tog, P1, turn.

Row 4 Slip the first stitch as if to purl with yarn in back, K7, slip 1 stitch as if to knit with yarn in back, K1, pass slipped stitch over, K1, turn.

Row 5 Slip the first stitch as if to purl with yarn in front, P8, P2tog, P1, turn.

Row 6 Slip the first stitch as if to purl with yarn in back, K9, slip 1 stitch as if to knit with yarn in back, K1, pass slipped stitch over, K1.

For Woman's small only: You now have 12 heel stitches; go to Knitting the Gusset.

For Woman's medium only:

Row 7 (wrong side) Slip the first stitch as if to purl with yarn in front, P10, P2tog, turn.

Row 8 Slip the first stitch as if to purl with yarn in back, K10, slip 1 stitch as if to knit with yarn in back, K1, pass slipped stitch over. *You now have* 12 heel stitches; go to Knitting the Gusset.

For Man's medium only:

Row 7 (wrong side) Slip the first stitch as if to purl with yarn in front, P10, P2tog, P1, turn.

Row 8 Slip the first stitch as if to purl with yarn in back, K10, slip 1 stitch as if to knit with yarn in back, K1, pass slipped stitch over, K1, turn.

Row 9 Slip the first stitch as if to purl with yarn in front, P11, P2tog, turn.

Row 10 Slip the first stitch as if to purl with yarn in back, K10, slip 1 stitch as if to knit with yarn in back, K1, pass slipped stitch over. *You now have* 12 heel stitches; go to Knitting the Gusset.

KNITTING THE GUSSET

Place all instep stitches on a single needle. Change to CC.

KNITTING THE GUSSET (CONT'D)	WOMAN'S SMALL	WOMAN'S MEDIUM	MAN'S MEDIUM
Set Up With right side facing and using the needle holding the heel stitches, pick up and knit along selvedge of heel flap	12 sts	12 sts	13 sts
With another needle, knit across from instep	18 sts	20 sts	22 sts
With a third needle, pick up and knit from other selvedge of heel flap	12 sts	12 sts	13 sts
Knit the first 6 stitches from heel needle onto the end of the third needle. *You now have*			
On Needle 1:	18 sts	18 sts	19 sts
On Needle 2:	18 sts	20 sts	22 sts
On Needle 3:	18 sts	18 sts	19 sts
Total stitches:	54 sts	56 sts	60 sts

Place marker to indicate beginning of round at center back heel. Continue in Stockinette Stitch while shaping gusset as follows:

Gusset Round 1

> Needle 1: Knit to last 3 stitches, K2tog, K1

> Needle 2: Knit

> Needle 3: K1, slip 1 stitch as if to knit with yarn in back, K1, pass slipped stitch over, knit to end: 2 stitches decreased, 1 stitch each from Needles 1 and 3.

Gusset Round 2 Knit.

	WOMAN'S SMALL	WOMAN'S MEDIUM	MAN'S MEDIUM
Repeat the last 2 rounds	8 more times	7 more times	7 more times
You now have	36 sts	40 sts	44 sts

KNITTING THE FOOT

	WOMAN'S SMALL	WOMAN'S MEDIUM	MAN'S MEDIUM
Continue in Stockinette Stitch until foot measures from center back heel about	6½" (16.5 cm)	7¾" (19.5 cm)	8½" (21.5 cm)
Or about this much less than desired total foot length:	1¾" (4.5 cm)	2¼" (5.5 cm)	2¼" (5.5 cm)

KNITTING THE TOE

Change to CB.

Toe Round 1

> Needle 1: Knit to last 3 stitches, K2tog, K1.

> Needle 2: K1, slip 1 stitch as if to knit with yarn in back, K1, pass slipped stitch over, knit to last 3 stitches, K2tog, K1.

> Needle 3: K1, slip 1 stitch as if to knit with yarn in back, K1, pass slipped stitch over, knit to end.

4 stitches decreased, 1 stitch each from Needles 1 and 3, and 2 stitches from Needle 2.

Toe Round 2 Knit.

KNITTING THE TOE (CONT'D)	WOMAN'S SMALL	WOMAN'S MEDIUM	MAN'S MEDIUM
Repeat the last 2 rounds	5 more times	6 more times	6 more times
You now have	12 sts	12 sts	16 sts
Place stitches from Needles 1 and 3 on one needle for bottom of toe. *You now have* on 2 needles	6 stitches each	6 stitches each	8 stitches each

FINISHING

Graft toe stitches together to close toe (see page 202).
 Weave in ends.

EMBROIDERY

Using a single strand of CA, work duplicate stitch embroidery (see page 194) around the inner edge of each large diamond as shown on embroidery chart for your size. Using a single strand of CB, work duplicate stitch around the center square of each diamond, then work duplicate stitch to fill the center of each small diamond. Using single strands of CA and CC, work alternating single duplicate stitches, checkerboard fashion, in the column(s) on the righthand side of the chart for your size.

Duplicate stitch outlining inner circle and emphasizing vertical "posts" on sock leg.

PERSIAN CARPET SOCKS CHARTS

KNITTING YARN COLORS

- ▪ CD FRENCH PUMPKIN
- ▪ CE COLEUS

EMBROIDERY YARN COLORS

- ▪ CA BLUE THYME
- ▪ CB PRETTY PINK
- ▪ CC MIDNIGHT BLUE

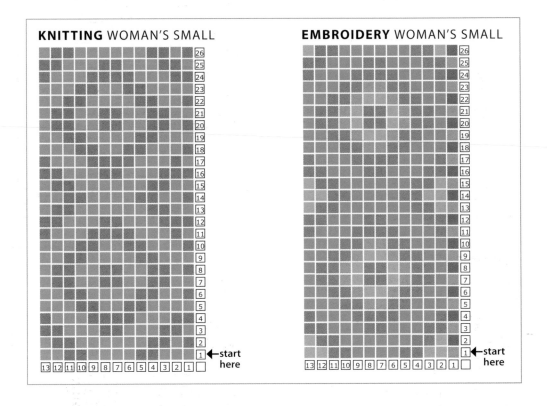

KNITTING WOMAN'S SMALL

EMBROIDERY WOMAN'S SMALL

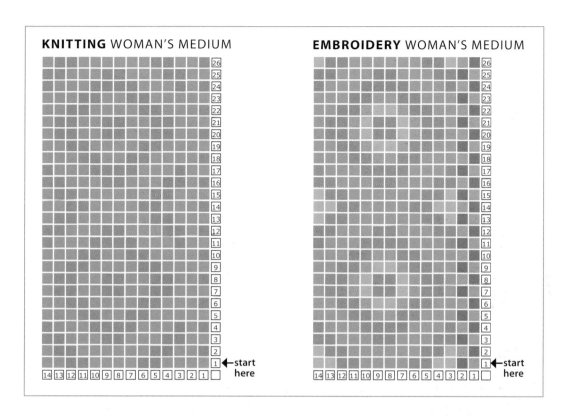

KNITTING WOMAN'S MEDIUM

26 25 24 23 22 21 20 19 18 17 16 15 14 13 12 11 10 9 8 7 6 5 4 3 2 1 ← start here

14 13 12 11 10 9 8 7 6 5 4 3 2 1

EMBROIDERY WOMAN'S MEDIUM

26 25 24 23 22 21 20 19 18 17 16 15 14 13 12 11 10 9 8 7 6 5 4 3 2 1 ← start here

14 13 12 11 10 9 8 7 6 5 4 3 2 1

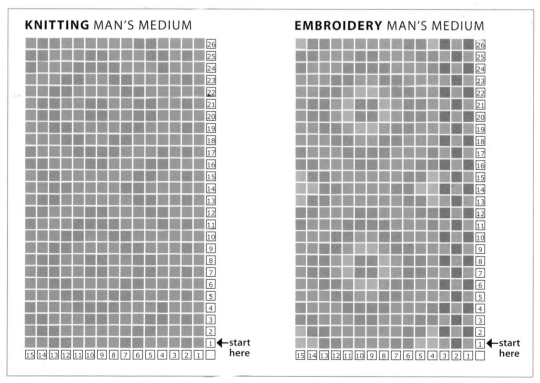

KNITTING MAN'S MEDIUM

26 25 24 23 22 21 20 19 18 17 16 15 14 13 12 11 10 9 8 7 6 5 4 3 2 1 ← start here

15 14 13 12 11 10 9 8 7 6 5 4 3 2 1

EMBROIDERY MAN'S MEDIUM

26 25 24 23 22 21 20 19 18 17 16 15 14 13 12 11 10 9 8 7 6 5 4 3 2 1 ← start here

15 14 13 12 11 10 9 8 7 6 5 4 3 2 1

Marvelous
MITTENS
& GLOVES

fingerless flower gloves

Knitting flowers into a fabric can be tedious if done using Fair Isle or intarsia methods. I've devised a much simpler way to get a knitted flower fix: Embroider them with chain and lazy daisy stitches, then top off with a separately knitted bobble for the flower center. They're a bit fussy and girly with their bobbled edges, but then sometimes that's just what you need.

Plan of action: The gloves are knitted in the round on double-pointed needles, using the smaller needles for the cuff and the larger for the hand. Both right and left gloves are knitted exactly the same. The placement of the embroidery on the back of the hand determines whether each finished glove is for a right or left hand.

stitches

BOBBLE EDGING
*P3, (K1, P1, K1, P1) all in same stitch to increase 1 stitch to 4 stitches, turn work so wrong side is facing, K4 bobble stitches, turn work so right side is facing, P4 bobble stitches, pass second, third, and fourth stitches on right needle over first stitch to decrease bobble back to 1 stitch; repeat from * to end of round.

GARTER RIDGE
Round 1 Knit.
Round 2 Purl.

K2, P2 RIB
Work all rounds as *K2, P2; repeat from * to end of round.

STOCKINETTE STITCH
Knit all stitches every round.

YARN

Nashua Handknits Julia, 50% wool/ 25% mohair/25% alpaca, 93 yd (85 m)/ 1¾ oz (50 g). Yarn band gauge: 5 stitches and 6 rows = 1" (2.5 cm) in Stockinette Stitch on US 7 (4.5 mm) needles.

CA = 8141 Pretty Pink, 1 skein for all sizes
CB = 3961 Ladies Mantle, 1 skein for all sizes
CC = 6086 Velvet Moss, 1 skein for all sizes
CD = 0178 Harvest Spice, 1 skein for all sizes

SIZES AND FINISHED HAND CIRCUMFERENCES

Child's medium, 6" (15 cm); Child's large/ Woman's small, 7" (18 cm); Woman's large/Man's small, 8" (20.5 cm); Man's large, 9" (23 cm)

Model shown in woman's large.

GAUGE

20 stitches and 26 rounds = 4" (10 cm) in Stockinette Stitch worked in the round using larger needle.

NEEDLES

Set of four US 7 (4.5 mm) double-pointed needles *or size you need to obtain the correct gauge*

Set of four US 6 (4 mm) double-pointed needles

NOTIONS

Tapestry needle

Stitch markers

Stitch holders

ABBREVIATIONS

K2tog = knit 2 stitches together

M1 = make 1 stitch

KNITTING THE CUFF	CHILD'S MEDIUM	CHILD'S LARGE/ WOMAN'S SMALL	WOMAN'S LARGE/MAN'S SMALL	MAN'S LARGE
Set Up Using CA and smaller needles, cast on	28 sts	32 sts	40 sts	44 sts
Divide stitches as evenly as possible on three needles. Place marker and join for working in the round, being careful not to twist stitches.				
Next Round Work 1 round for Bobble Edging.				
Next 2 Rounds Work 1 Garter Ridge.				
Next 2 Rounds Change to CB and work 1 Garter Ridge.				
Next Round Change to CC and knit 1 round.				
Next Rounds Work in K2, P2 Rib until ribbing measures above last Garter Ridge	2¼" (5.5 cm)	2½" (6.5 cm)	3" (7.5 cm)	3¼" (8.5 cm)
Next 2 Rounds Change to CA and work 1 Garter Ridge.				
Next Round Change to CB and knit, increasing evenly	2 sts	4 sts	0 sts	2 sts
You now have	30 sts	36 sts	40 sts	46 sts
Next Round Purl.				
Cuff measures from cast on about	3¼" (8.5 cm)	3½" (9 cm)	4" (10 cm)	4¼" (11 cm)
KNITTING THE HAND				
Change to CD and larger needles. Work even in Stockinette Stitch	1 rnd	2 rnds	3 rnds	4 rnds
Next Round				
Knit	15 sts	18 sts	20 sts	23 sts
Place marker for thumb gusset.				
M1 (see page 200).				
Place marker for thumb gusset.				
Knit	15 sts	18 sts	20 sts	23 sts
You now have	31 sts	37 sts	41 sts	47 sts
You now have 1 stitch between the gusset markers for all sizes.				
Next Round Knit 1 round even for all sizes.				
Next Round (increase round) Knit to first thumb gusset marker, slip marker, M1, knit to second thumb gusset marker, M1, slip marker, knit to end: 2 stitches increased between gusset markers.				

KNITTING THE HAND (CONT'D)	CHILD'S MEDIUM	CHILD'S LARGE/ WOMAN'S SMALL	WOMAN'S LARGE/MAN'S SMALL	MAN'S LARGE
Next Rounds Repeat the last 2 rounds	4 more times	5 more times	6 more times	7 more times
You now have	41 sts	49 sts	55 sts	63 sts
You now have between the gusset markers	11 sts	13 sts	15 sts	17 sts
Next Round Knit to first gusset marker, remove marker, place gusset stitches on holder, remove second gusset marker, knit to end.				
You now have	30 sts	36 sts	40 sts	46 sts
Next Rounds Work even in Stockinette Stitch until glove reaches base of pinky finger, or until stockinette section measures above last Garter Ridge about	3½" (9 cm)	4" (10 cm)	4½" (11.5 cm)	5" (12.5 cm)
Next 2 Rounds Change to CB and work 1 Garter Ridge.				
Next Round				
Child's medium only: *K4, K2tog; repeat from * to end.				
Child's large/Woman's small only: *K4, K2tog; repeat from * to end.				
Woman's large/Man's small only: *K4, K2tog; repeat from * to last 4 stitches, K4.				
Man's large only: *K4, K2tog; repeat from * to last 4 stitches, K4.				
You now have	25 sts	30 sts	34 sts	39 sts
Next Round Purl.				
Change to CA and bind off all stitches neatly.				
KNITTING THE THUMB				
Place held stitches from thumb gusset on 2 needles. Join CD to beginning of thumb stitches with right side facing. Knit across thumb stitches, then pick up and knit 1 stitch from base of hole where hand stitches rejoined for working in the round.				
You now have	12 sts	14 sts	16 sts	18 sts
Divide stitches as evenly as possible among three needles.				
Next 2 Rounds Change to CB and work 1 Garter Ridge.				

KNITTING THE THUMB (CONT'D)	CHILD'S MEDIUM	CHILD'S LARGE/ WOMAN'S SMALL	WOMAN'S LARGE/MAN'S SMALL	MAN'S LARGE
Next Round				
Child's medium only: *K3, K2tog; repeat from * to last 2 stitches, K2.				
Child's large/Woman's small only: *K3, K2tog; repeat from * to last 4 stitches, K4.				
Woman's large/Man's small only: *K3, K2tog; repeat from * to last stitch, K1.				
Man's large only: *K3, K2tog; repeat from * to last 3 stitches, K3.				
You now have	10 sts	12 sts	13 sts	15 sts
Next Round Purl.				
Change to CA and bind off all stitches neatly.				

FINISHING

Weave in ends. Use yarn tail at base of thumb to close any remaining hole where thumb meets hand.

BOBBLES FOR FLOWER CENTERS

Note   Make sure to work the flowers on the opposite side for each glove so you will have both a right and left hand. Make 4 bobbles using CA, following the directions for Knitting the Bobbles below.

knitting the bobbles

Set Up   Cast on 1 stitch.

Row 1 (right side)   Knit into the front, back, front, and back of same stitch to make 4 stitches from the single cast-on stitch.

Rows 2 and 4 (wrong side)   P4.

Row 3   K4.

Row 5   K4, pass second, third, and fourth stitches over first stitch to decrease back to 1 stitch.

Cut yarn, leaving a 5" (12.5 cm) tail, and fasten off last stitch. With purl side of the bobble facing out, tie cast on and bind off tails together. Attach two bobbles to back of each hand, leaving enough room around bobbles for flower petals. Weave tails into center of bobbles as stuffing to create rounded shapes, and attach to back of glove.

EMBROIDERY

Using a single strand of CC, embroider two curving stems using chain stitch (see page 197) on the back of each glove, starting at the top of the Garter Ridge, and ending at a bobble as shown.

With single strand of CC, embroider leaves on either side of the stems using individual lazy daisy stitches (see page 197).

Using a single strand of CB, work different sized petals in lazy daisy stitch around each bobble as shown.

Flowers worked in chain and lazy daisy stitches, with knit bobble centers.

olivia's and celia's mittens

My two nieces Olivia and Celia made these mittens for me. They used two different cuff treatments. The blue cuff of Olivia's mitten (version 1) is edged with garter ridges and made snug by simple 2 × 2 ribbing. Lazy daisy flowers with French knots decorate the main part of the mitten. Celia's pink mittens (version 2) are edged with a solid green band of Garter Ridges and stockinette stitch. Eyelets make holes to slip the pompom-trimmed tie through. Easy French knots decorate the stripes, giving the mittens a polka dot feel.

Plan of action: The mittens are knitted in the round on double-pointed needles. You use the smaller needles for the ribbed cuff and switch to the larger ones for the hand. Both right and left mittens are knit exactly the same and can be worn on either hand.

stitches

GARTER RIDGE
Round 1 Knit.
Round 2 Purl.

K2, P2 RIB
Work all rounds as *K2, P2; repeat from * to end of round.

STOCKINETTE STITCH
Knit all stitches every round.

STRIPE PATTERN
Rounds 1–4 Knit 4 rounds with darker stripe color.
Rounds 5–8 Knit 4 rounds with lighter stripe color.
Repeat these 8 rounds for stripe pattern.

YARN

Nashua Handknits Julia, 50% wool/25% mohair/25% alpaca, 93 yd (85 m)/1¾ oz (50 g). Yarn band gauge: 5 stitches and 6 rows = 1" (2.5 cm) in Stockinette Stitch on US 7 (4.5 mm) needles.

Version 1:
CA = 2163 Golden Honey, 1 skein for all sizes
CB = 0178 Harvest Spice, 1 skein for all sizes
CC = 3983 Delphinium, 1 skein for all sizes
CD = 5178 Lupine, 1 skein for all sizes

Version 2:
CA = 5185 Spring Green, 1 skein for all sizes
CB = 6085 Deep Geranium, 1 skein for all sizes
CC = 8141 Pretty Pink, 1 skein for all sizes

Note To make solid-colored mittens, follow these directions, but omit the striping. Remember, purchase twice as much yarn of the main color.

SIZES AND FINISHED HAND CIRCUMFERENCES

Child's medium, 6" (15 cm); Child's large/Woman's small, 7" (18 cm); Woman's large/Man's small, 8" (20.5 cm); Man's large, 9" (23 cm)

Models shown are child's large/woman's small (version 1) and woman's large/man's small (version 2).

GAUGE

20 stitches and 26 rounds = 4" (10 cm) in Stockinette Stitch worked in the round using larger needle.

NEEDLES

Set of four US 7 (4.5 mm) double-pointed needles *or size you need to obtain the correct gauge*

Set of four US 6 (4 mm) double-pointed needles

NOTIONS

Tapestry needle

Stitch markers

Stitch holders

Pompom maker (optional) or scrap cardboard for Version 2

ABBREVIATIONS

K2tog = knit 2 stitches together
M1 = make 1 stitch (see page 200)
YO = Yarnover

KNITTING VERSION 1	CHILD'S MEDIUM	CHILD'S LARGE/ WOMAN'S SMALL	WOMAN'S LARGE/ MAN'S SMALL	MAN'S LARGE
Cuff				
Set Up Using CA and smaller needles, cast on	28 sts	32 sts	40 sts	44 sts
Divide stitches as evenly as possible on three needles. Place marker and join for working in the round, being careful not to twist stitches.				
Next Round Purl.				
Next 2 Rounds Work 1 Garter Ridge.				
Next Round Change to CB and knit 1 round.				
Next Rounds Work in K2, P2 Rib until ribbing measures above last Garter Ridge	2" (5 cm)	2½" (6.5 cm)	2¾" (4.5 cm)	3" (7.5 cm)
Next 4 Rounds Change to CA and work 2 Garter Ridges.				
Hand				
Change to larger needles and CC.				
Next Round Knit, increasing evenly	2 sts	3 sts	0 sts	1 sts
You now have	30 sts	35 sts	40 sts	45 sts
Next Rounds Begin working in Stripe Pattern, using CC for the darker stripe color and CD for the lighter stripe color, and counting the increase round just worked as Round 1 of the first dark stripe. Work even in Stripe Pattern until mitten measures from cast-on edge	3¼" (8.5 cm)	3¾" (9.5 cm)	4½" (11.5 cm)	5" (12.5 cm)
Next Round				
Knit	15 sts	18 sts	20 sts	23 sts
Place marker for thumb gusset.				
M1 (see page 200).				
Place marker for thumb gusset.				
Knit	15 sts	17 sts	20 sts	22 sts
You now have	31 sts	36 sts	41 sts	46 sts
You now have 1 stitch between the gusset markers for all sizes.				
Next Round Knit 1 round even for all sizes.				
Next Round (increase round) Knit to first thumb gusset marker, slip marker, M1, knit to second thumb gusset marker, M1, slip marker, knit to end: 2 stitches increased between gusset markers.				

KNITTING VERSION 1 (CONT'D)	CHILD'S MEDIUM	CHILD'S LARGE/ WOMAN'S SMALL	WOMAN'S LARGE/ MAN'S SMALL	MAN'S LARGE
Next Rounds Repeat the last 2 rounds	4 more times	5 more times	6 more times	7 more times
You now have	41 sts	48 sts	55 sts	62 sts
You now have between the gusset markers	11 sts	13 sts	15 sts	17 sts
Next Round Knit to first gusset marker, remove marker, place gusset stitches on holder, remove second gusset marker, knit to end. *You now have*	30 sts	35 sts	40 sts	45 sts
Next Rounds Work even in Stripe Pattern until mitten reaches tip of index finger, or until Stripe Pattern section measures above last Garter Ridge about	4½" (11.5 cm)	6¼" (16 cm)	6½" (16.5 cm)	7" (18 cm)

Continue Stripe Pattern while shaping top of hand as follows:

Next Round

Child's medium only: *K2, K2tog; repeat from * to last 2 stitches, K2.

Child's large/Woman's small only: *K2, K2tog; repeat from * to last 3 stitches, K3.

Woman's large/Man's small only: *K2, K2tog; repeat from * to end.

Man's large only: *K2, K2tog; repeat from * to last stitch, K1.

	CHILD'S MEDIUM	CHILD'S LARGE/ WOMAN'S SMALL	WOMAN'S LARGE/ MAN'S SMALL	MAN'S LARGE
You now have	23 sts	27 sts	30 sts	34 sts

Next Round Knit.

Next Round

Child's medium only: *K1, K2tog; repeat from * to last 2 stitches, K2.

Child's large/Woman's small only: *K1, K2tog; repeat from * to end.

Woman's large/Man's small only: *K1, K2tog; repeat from * to end.

Man's large only: *K1, K2tog; repeat from * to last 4 stitches, K2tog twice.

	CHILD'S MEDIUM	CHILD'S LARGE/ WOMAN'S SMALL	WOMAN'S LARGE/ MAN'S SMALL	MAN'S LARGE
You now have	16 sts	18 sts	20 sts	22 sts

Next Round Knit.

Next Round *K2tog; repeat from * to end. *You now have*	8 sts	9 sts	10 sts	11 sts

Next Round

Child's medium only: *K2tog; repeat from * to end.

KNITTING VERSION 1 (CONT'D)	CHILD'S MEDIUM	CHILD'S LARGE/ WOMAN'S SMALL	WOMAN'S LARGE/ MAN'S SMALL	MAN'S LARGE
Child's large/Woman's small only: *K2tog; repeat from * to last stitch, K1.				
Woman's large/Man's small only: *K2tog; repeat from * to end.				
Man's large only: *K2tog; repeat from * to last stitch, K1.				
You now have	4 sts	5 sts	5 sts	6 sts
Cut yarn leaving a 10" (25.5 cm) tail. Thread tail on tapestry needle and run through all stitches like a drawstring. Pull tail firmly to close top of hand, and weave in tail on wrong side.				

Thumb

	CHILD'S MEDIUM	CHILD'S LARGE/ WOMAN'S SMALL	WOMAN'S LARGE/ MAN'S SMALL	MAN'S LARGE
Place held stitches from thumb gusset on 2 needles. Join yarn color that matches hand stripe to beginning of thumb stitches with right side facing. Knit across thumb stitches, then pick up and knit 1 stitch from base of hole where hand stitches rejoined for working in the round. *You now have*	12 sts	14 sts	16 sts	18 sts
Divide stitches as evenly as possible on three needles. Work even in established Stripe Pattern to match hand until thumb measures	1" (2.5 cm)	1¼" (3.2 cm)	1¾" (4.5 cm)	2" (5 cm)

Next Round

	CHILD'S MEDIUM	CHILD'S LARGE/ WOMAN'S SMALL	WOMAN'S LARGE/ MAN'S SMALL	MAN'S LARGE
Child's medium only: *K2tog, K2; repeat from * to end.				
Child's large/Woman's small only: *K2tog, K2; repeat from * to last 2 stitches, K2.				
Woman's large/Man's small only: *K2tog, K2; repeat from * to end.				
Man's large only: *K2tog, K2; repeat from * to last 2 stitches, K2.				
You now have	9 sts	11 sts	12 sts	14 sts

Next Round

	CHILD'S MEDIUM	CHILD'S LARGE/ WOMAN'S SMALL	WOMAN'S LARGE/ MAN'S SMALL	MAN'S LARGE
Child's medium only: *K2tog, K1; repeat from * to end.				
Child's large/Woman's small only: *K2tog, K1; repeat from * to last 2 stitches, K2.				
Woman's large/Man's small only: *K2tog, K1; repeat from * to end.				
Man's large only: *K2tog, K1; repeat from * to last 2 stitches, K2.				
You now have	6 sts	8 sts	8 sts	10 sts

KNITTING VERSION 1 (CONT'D)	CHILD'S MEDIUM	CHILD'S LARGE/ WOMAN'S SMALL	WOMAN'S LARGE/ MAN'S SMALL	MAN'S LARGE
Next Round *K2tog; repeat from * to end.				
You now have	3 sts	4 sts	4 sts	5 sts
Cut yarn leaving a 10" (25.5 cm) tail. Thread tail on tapestry needle and run through all stitches like a drawstring. Pull tail firmly to close top of thumb, and weave in tail on wrong side.				

FINISHING

Weave in ends. Use the yarn tail at base of thumb to close up any remaining hole where the thumb meets the hand.

EMBROIDERY

Using a single strand of CA, on each side of hand embroider four six-petaled flowers using lazy daisy stitch (see page 197) as shown.

With single strand of CB, embroider a French knot (see page 197) in the center of each flower as shown.

Flowers worked in French knots and lazy daisy stitches.

KNITTING VERSION 2	CHILD'S MEDIUM	CHILD'S LARGE/ WOMAN'S SMALL	WOMAN'S LARGE/ MAN'S SMALL	MAN'S LARGE
Cuff				
Set Up Using CA and smaller needles, cast on	30 sts	35 sts	40 sts	45 sts
Divide stitches as evenly as possible on three needles. Place marker and join for working in the round, being careful not to twist stitches.				
Next Round Purl.				
Next 2 Rounds Work 1 Garter Ridge.				
Next Round Knit.				
Next Round Work eyelet holes for wrist ties as follows:				
Child's medium only: [K2, K2tog, YO] 5 times, K1, K2tog, YO, K2, K2tog, YO, K1, K2tog, YO.				

KNITTING VERSION 2 (CONT'D)	CHILD'S MEDIUM	CHILD'S LARGE/ WOMAN'S SMALL	WOMAN'S LARGE/ MAN'S SMALL	MAN'S LARGE
Child's large/Woman's small only: [K2, K2tog, YO, K3, K2tog, YO] 3 times, [K2, K2tog, YO] 2 times.				
Woman's large/Man's small only: [K1, K2tog, YO, K1] 10 times.				
Man's large only: [K2, K2tog, YO, K3, K2tog, YO] 4 times, K3, K2tog, YO, K2, K2tog, YO.				
You now have	8 eyelet holes	8 eyelet holes	10 eyelet holes	10 eyelet holes
Next 4 Rounds Work 2 Garter Ridges.				
Hand				
Change to CB and begin working in Stripe Pattern, using CB for the darker stripe color and CC for the lighter stripe color. Work even in Stripe Pattern until mitten measures from cast-on edge	3¼" (8.5 cm)	3¾" (9.5 cm)	4½" (11.5 cm)	5" (12.5 cm)
Complete hand and work thumb as for Version 1.				

FINISHING

Weave in ends. Use the yarn tail at base of thumb to close up any remaining hole where the thumb meets the hand.

EMBROIDERY

Using a double strand of CA, embroider lines of French knots (see page 197) where the stripe color changes from dark to light (every other color change) as shown in the photo on page 74, placing knots with about 3 knit stitches between each pair of knots. Do not cut CA between the knots. Instead, carry the yarn loosely along the wrong side of the mitten to the next French knot position.

French knots every fourth stitch, placed at color changes.

TIES

With larger needles and CC, cast on 50 stitches. Bind off all stitches on next row.

Make a second tie the same as the first. Weave in ends of ties.

Beginning at the edge of the hand beneath the pinky finger, weave a tie in and out of the eyelet holes all the way around each wrist.

POMPOMS

Make four pompoms (see page 199) in the colors of your choice. I used equal amounts of two colors for each of the pompoms shown (two with CA and CB, and two with CA and CC). Attach pompoms to the ends of ties.

dots-and-checks mittens

f air Isle knitting can be so intimidating for a beginner knitter, but once you try it, you'll be hooked. Knitting small Fair Isle patterns like dots and checks is soothing, not stressful. The pattern builds quickly on your needles, and before you know it, you'll have the sequence memorized and the mittens will be finished! Pick some fun colors to create your own little knit bit of optical art. And who says mittens have to match?

Plan of action: You choose whether to work a ruffled or a plain edge to the cuffs and then whether to follow the chart for dots or checks on the hands. (See pages 191 and 195 for instructions on working from a chart.) In either case, you start with the smaller needles for the cuffs and switch to the larger ones for the hands. Both right and left mittens are knitted exactly the same and can be worn on either hand.

stitches

> **GARTER RIDGE**
> **Round 1** Knit.
> **Round 2** Purl.
>
> **STOCKINETTE STITCH**
> Knit all stitches every round.

YARN

Nashua Handknits Julia, 50% wool/ 25% mohair/25% alpaca, 93 yd (85 m)/ 1¾ oz (50 g). Yarn band gauge: 5 stitches and 6 rows = 1" (2.5 cm) in Stockinette Stitch on US 7 (4.5 mm) needles.

Dots Mittens:
CA = 5185 Spring Green, 1 skein for all sizes
CB = 2083 Magenta, 1 skein for all sizes
CC = 4936 Blue Thyme, 1 skein for all sizes

Checks Mittens:
CA = 2083 Magenta, 1 skein for all sizes
CB = 4330 Mushroom, 1 skein for all sizes
CC = 2250 French Pumpkin, 1 skein for all sizes
CD = 4345 Coleus, 1 skein for all sizes

SIZES AND FINISHED HAND CIRCUMFERENCES

Child's small, 5½" (14 cm); Child's medium, 6½" (16.5 cm); Woman's medium, 7¼" (18.5); Woman's large/ Man's small, 8¼" (21 cm)

Models shown are Woman's medium in Dots, and Woman's large/Man's small in Checks.

GAUGE

22 stitches and 24 rounds = 4" (10 cm) in Stockinette Stitch colorwork pattern from charts worked in the round using larger needles.

NEEDLES

Set of four US 6 (4 mm) double-pointed needles *or size you need to obtain the correct gauge*

Set of four US 5 (3.75 mm) double-pointed needles

US 6 (4 mm) circular needle 24" (60 cm) long (optional for ruffled edging)

ABBREVIATIONS

K2tog = knit 2 stitches together

M1 = make 1 stitch (see page 200)

NOTIONS

Tapestry needle

Stitch markers

Stitch holders

KNITTING THE CUFF	CHILD'S SMALL	CHILD'S MEDIUM	WOMAN'S MEDIUM	WOMAN'S LARGE/ MAN'S SMALL
Begin by working the cuff of your choice, either with a ruffled or plain edge.				
Ruffled Edge				
Set Up Using CA and larger circular needle, cast on Do not join for working in the round.	90 sts	105 sts	120 sts	135 sts
Row 1 (wrong side) Purl.				
Row 2 (right side) *Slip 1 stitch as if to knit, K2tog, pass slipped stitch over; repeat from * to end. *You now have*	30 sts	35 sts	40 sts	45 sts
Row 3 (wrong side) Change to CB and purl 1 row.				
Using smaller double-pointed needles, divide stitches as evenly as possible on three needles with the right (knit) side of the ruffle on the outside of the round. Place marker and join for working in the round, being careful not to twist stitches.				
Round 4 Purl 1 round to complete first Garter Ridge above ruffle.				
Rounds 5 and 6 Change to CC and work 1 Garter Ridge.				
Rounds 7 and 8 Change to CB and work 1 Garter Ridge.				
Rounds 9–12 Repeat Rounds 5–8 once more.				
Rounds 13 and 14 Repeat Rounds 5 and 6 once more: 6 Garter Ridges completed above ruffle.				
Go to Knitting the Hand.				
Plain Edge				
Set Up Using CA and smaller needles, cast on	30 sts	35 sts	40 sts	45 sts
Divide stitches as evenly as possible on three needles. Place marker and join for working in the round, being careful not to twist stitches.				
Round 1 Purl 1 round to complete first Garter Ridge.				
Rounds 2 and 3 Change to CB and work 1 Garter Ridge.				
Rounds 4 and 5 Change to CA and work 1 Garter Ridge.				

KNITTING THE CUFF (CONT'D)	CHILD'S SMALL	CHILD'S MEDIUM	WOMAN'S MEDIUM	WOMAN'S LARGE/ MAN'S SMALL
Rounds 6–9 Repeat Rounds 2–5 once more.				
Rounds 10 and 11 Repeat Rounds 2 and 3 once more: 6 Garter Ridges completed.				
Go to Knitting the Hand.				

KNITTING THE HAND

	CHILD'S SMALL	CHILD'S MEDIUM	WOMAN'S MEDIUM	WOMAN'S LARGE/ MAN'S SMALL
Change to larger needles.				
Next Rounds Work in pattern from either the Dots or Checks Chart until mitten measures from cast-on edge	2½" (6.5 cm)	2½" (6.5 cm)	3" (7.5 cm)	3½" (9 cm)
Next Round Work in pattern	15 sts	17 sts	20 sts	22 sts
Place marker for thumb gusset.				
M1 (see page 200) using CA for Dots pattern or CC for Checks pattern.				
Place marker for thumb gusset.				
Work in pattern	15 sts	18 sts	20 sts	23 sts
You now have	31 sts	36 sts	41 sts	46 sts
You now have 1 stitch between the gusset markers for all sizes.				
Next Round Work 1 round even in pattern, working increased stitch using its matching color.				
Next Round (increase round) Work in pattern to first thumb gusset marker, slip marker, M1 using CB for Dots pattern or CD for Checks pattern, knit to second thumb gusset marker, M1 using CB for Dots pattern or CD for Checks pattern, slip marker, work in pattern to end: 2 stitches increased between gusset markers.				
Next Round Work 1 round even in pattern, working all thumb gusset stitches in the colors as they appear.				
Next Round (increase round) Work in pattern to first thumb gusset marker, slip marker, M1 using CA for Dots pattern or CC for Checks pattern, knit to second thumb gusset marker, M1 using CA for Dots pattern or CC for Checks pattern, slip marker, work in pattern to end: 2 stitches increased between gusset markers.				
Next Round Work 1 round even in pattern, working all thumb gusset stitches in the colors as they appear.				
Next Rounds Repeat the last 4 rounds	1 more time	2 more times	2 more times	3 more times

KNITTING THE HAND (CONT'D)	CHILD'S SMALL	CHILD'S MEDIUM	WOMAN'S MEDIUM	WOMAN'S LARGE/ MAN'S SMALL
You now have	39 sts	48 sts	53 sts	62 sts
You now have between the gusset markers	9 sts	13 sts	13 sts	17 sts
For sizes Child's small and Woman's medium only: Work 2 more rounds as follows:				
Next Round (increase round) Work in pattern to first thumb gusset marker, slip marker, M1 using CB for Dots pattern or CD for Checks pattern, knit to second thumb gusset marker, M1 using CB for Dots pattern or CD for Checks pattern, slip marker, work in pattern to end: 2 stitches increased between gusset markers.				
Next Round Work 1 round even in pattern, working all thumb gusset stitches in the colors as they appear. *You now have*	41 sts	48 sts	55 sts	62 sts
You now have between the gusset markers	11 sts	13 sts	15 sts	17 sts
Next Round Work in pattern to first gusset marker, remove marker, place gusset stitches on holder, remove second gusset marker, work in pattern to end. *You now have*	30 sts	35 sts	40 sts	45 sts
Next Rounds Work even in pattern until mitten reaches tip of index finger, or from beginning (first increase round) of thumb gusset measures about	3" (7.5 cm)	4¼" (11 cm)	5¼" (14 cm)	6½" (16.5 cm)
End having just finished an entire dot or check.				
Next Round Change to CB for Dots pattern or CC for Checks pattern and knit 1 round.				
Next Round Work in solid color Stockinette while shaping top of hand as follows:				
Child's small only: *K2, K2tog; repeat from * to last 2 stitches, K2.				
Child's medium only: *K2, K2tog; repeat from * to last 3 stitches, K3.				
Woman's medium only: *K2, K2tog; repeat from * to end.				
Woman's large/Man's small only: *K2, K2tog; repeat from * to last stitch, K1.				
You now have	23 sts	27 sts	30 sts	34 sts
Next Round Knit.				
Next Round				
Child's small only: *K1, K2tog; repeat from * to last 2 stitches, K2.				

KNITTING THE HAND (CONT'D)	CHILD'S SMALL	CHILD'S MEDIUM	WOMAN'S MEDIUM	WOMAN'S LARGE/ MAN'S SMALL
Child's medium only: *K1, K2tog; repeat from * to end.				
Woman's medium only: *K1, K2tog; repeat from * to end.				
Woman's large/Man's small only: *K1, K2tog; repeat from * to last 4 stitches, K2tog twice.				
You now have	16 sts	18 sts	20 sts	22 sts
Next Round Knit.				
Next Round *K2tog; repeat from * to end.				
You now have	8 sts	9 sts	10 sts	11 sts
Next Round				
Child's small only: *K2tog; repeat from * to end.				
Child's medium only: *K2tog; repeat from * to last stitch, K1.				
Woman's medium only: *K2tog; repeat from * to end.				
Woman's large/Man's small only: *K2tog; repeat from * to last stitch, K1.				
You now have	4 sts	5 sts	5 sts	6 sts
Cut yarn leaving a 10" (25.5 cm) tail. Thread tail on tapestry needle and run through all stitches like a drawstring. Pull tail firmly to close top of hand, and weave in tail on wrong side.				

KNITTING THE THUMB

	CHILD'S SMALL	CHILD'S MEDIUM	WOMAN'S MEDIUM	WOMAN'S LARGE/ MAN'S SMALL
Place held stitches from thumb gusset on 2 larger double-pointed needles. Join CB for Dots pattern or CC for Checks pattern to beginning of thumb stitches with right side facing. Knit across thumb stitches, then pick up and knit 1 stitch from base of hole where hand stitches rejoined for working in the round. *You now have*	12 sts	14 sts	16 sts	18 sts
Divide stitches as evenly as possible among three needles. Work even in solid color Stockinette until thumb measures	1" (2.5 cm)	1¼" (3.2 cm)	1½" (3.8 cm)	2" (5 cm)
Next Round				
Child's small only: *K2tog, K2; repeat from * to end.				
Child's medium only: *K2tog, K2; repeat from * to last 2 stitches, K2.				
Woman's medium only: *K2tog, K2; repeat from * to end.				

KNITTING THE THUMB (CONT'D)	CHILD'S SMALL	CHILD'S MEDIUM	WOMAN'S MEDIUM	WOMAN'S LARGE/ MAN'S SMALL
Woman's large/Man's small only: *K2tog, K2; repeat from * to last 2 stitches, K2.				
You now have	9 sts	11 sts	12 sts	14 sts
Next Round				
Child's small only: *K2tog, K1; repeat from * to end.				
Child's medium only: *K2tog, K1; repeat from * to last 2 stitches, K2.				
Woman's medium only: *K2tog, K1; repeat from * to end.				
Woman's large/Man's small only: *K2tog, K1; repeat from * to last 2 stitches, K2.				
You now have	6 sts	8 sts	8 sts	10 sts
Next Round *K2tog; repeat from * to end. You now have*	3 sts	4 sts	4 sts	5 sts
Cut yarn leaving a 10" (25.5 cm) tail. Thread tail on tapestry needle and run through all stitches like a drawstring. Pull tail firmly to close top of thumb, and weave in tail on wrong side.				
FINISHING				

Weave in ends. Use the yarn tail at base of thumb to close up any remaining hole where the thumb meets the hand.

DOTS-AND-CHECKS MITTENS CHARTS

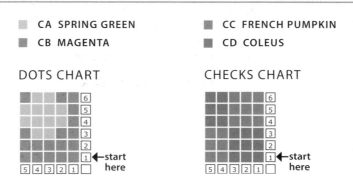

- CA SPRING GREEN
- CB MAGENTA
- CC FRENCH PUMPKIN
- CD COLEUS

DOTS CHART   CHECKS CHART

nordic-inspired mittens

When I was girl, my mother knit me a pair of Norwegian snowflake mittens. I watched her for hours (and seasons, for she wasn't the quickest knitter and she had five daughters to care for!) as the mittens grew on four needles. To me, it was sheer magic, seeing the pattern lengthen and then diminish into a pointed tip. I couldn't wait to wear them, knowing that the double thickness of yarn would withstand any snowball fight. These mittens are my homage to my mom's patient hours and to all Nordic knitters who continue to inspire me with their creativity and art. My color choice isn't traditional, and to make them even more over the edge, I decorated the seed stitch border with pumpkin-colored French knots.

Plan of action: The cuffs are knitted in Seed Stitch using the smaller needles. Then you change to the larger needles and follow the Nordic-Inspired Mittens Chart for the hands. (See pages 191 and 195 for instructions on following a chart.) French knots add further decoration at the end. Both right and left mittens are knitted exactly the same and can be worn on either hand.

stitches

> **SEED STITCH**
> **(EVEN NUMBER OF STITCHES)**
> **Round 1** *K1, P1; repeat from * to end.
> **Round 2** *P1, K1; repeat from * to end.
>
> **STOCKINETTE STITCH**
> Knit all stitches every round.

YARN

Nashua Handknits Julia, 50% wool/ 25% mohair/25% alpaca, 93 yd (85 m)/ 1¾ oz (50 g). Yarn band gauge: 5 stitches and 6 rows = 1" (2.5 cm) in Stockinette Stitch on US 7 (4.5 mm) needles.

CA = 4345 Coleus, 2 skeins for all sizes

CB = 3961 Ladies Mantle, 1 skein for all sizes

CC = 2250 French Pumpkin, 1 skein for all sizes

SIZES AND FINISHED HAND CIRCUMFERENCES

Child's large/Woman's small, 6¾" (17 cm); Woman's large, 8½" (21.5 cm); Man's large, 9¼" (23.5 cm)

Model shown in woman's large.

GAUGE

20 stitches and 21 rounds = 4" (10 cm) in Stockinette Stitch colorwork pattern from chart worked in the round using larger needles.

NEEDLES

Set of four US 7 (4.5 mm) double-pointed needles *or size you need to obtain the correct gauge*

Set of four US 6 (4 mm) double-pointed needles

NOTIONS

Tapestry needle

Stitch markers

Stitch holders

ABBREVIATIONS

K2tog = knit 2 stitches together

M1 = make 1 (see page 200)

Ssk = slip, slip, knit these 2 stitches together

KNITTING THE CUFF	CHILD'S LARGE/ WOMAN'S SMALL	WOMAN'S LARGE	MAN'S LARGE
Set Up Using CA and smaller needles, cast on	34 sts	42 sts	46 sts

Divide stitches as evenly as possible on three needles. Place marker and join for working in the round, being careful not to twist stitches.

Next Rounds Work in Seed Stitch until piece measures 1" (2.5 cm) from cast-on edge.

KNITTING THE HAND			
Change to larger needles. **Note** One pattern repeat of the Nordic-Inspired Mittens Chart contains	17 sts	21 sts	23 sts

Using CA and CB as shown, repeat the Nordic-Inspired Mittens Chart for your size 2 times for each round.

Next Rounds Work in pattern from Nordic-Inspired Mittens Chart for your size until mitten measures from cast on edge	3" (7.5 cm)	4" (10 cm)	4" (10 cm)

Next Round

Work in pattern	17 sts	21 sts	23 sts

Place marker for thumb gusset. M1 (see page 200) using CA. Place marker for thumb gusset.

Work in pattern	17 sts	21 sts	23 sts
You now have	35 sts	43 sts	47 sts

You now have 1 stitch between the gusset markers for all sizes.

Next Round Work 1 round even in pattern, working increased stitch, using its matching color.

Next Round (increase round) Work in pattern to first thumb gusset marker, slip marker, M1 using CB, knit to second thumb gusset marker, M1 using CB, slip marker, work in pattern to end: 2 stitches increased between gusset markers.

Next Round Work 1 round even in pattern, working all thumb gusset stitches in the colors as they appear.

Next Round (increase round) Work in pattern to first thumb gusset marker, slip marker, M1 using CA, knit to second thumb gusset marker, M1 using CA, slip marker, work in pattern to end: 2 stitches increased between gusset markers.

Next Round Work 1 round even in pattern, working all thumb gusset stitches in the colors as they appear.

Next Rounds Repeat the last 4 rounds	2 more times	2 more times	3 more times
You now have	47 sts	55 sts	63 sts
You now have between the gusset markers	13 sts	13 sts	17 sts

KNITTING THE HAND (CONT'D)	CHILD'S LARGE/ WOMAN'S SMALL	WOMAN'S LARGE	MAN'S LARGE
For Woman's large only: Work 2 more rounds as follows:			
Next Round (increase round) Work in pattern to first thumb gusset marker, slip marker, M1 using CB, knit to second thumb gusset marker, M1 using CB, work in pattern to end: 2 stitches increased between gusset markers.			
Next Round Work 1 round even in pattern, working all thumb gusset stitches in the colors as they appear.			
You now have	47 sts	57 sts	63 sts
You now have between the gusset markers	13 sts	15 sts	17 sts
Next Round Work in pattern to first gusset marker, remove marker, place gusset stitches on holder, remove second gusset marker, work in pattern to end.			
You now have	34 sts	42 sts	46 sts
Next Rounds Work even in pattern from chart for your size until you have completed from the beginning of the Nordic-Inspired Mittens Chart	35 rounds	45 rounds	50 rounds
End having just finished	Round 7	Round 9	Round 10
Mitten measures from beginning of Nordic-Inspired Mittens Chart about	6¾" (17 cm)	8½" (21.5 cm)	9½" (24 cm)
Rearrange stitches as follows, slipping stitches from one needle to another without working them:			
On Needle 1	17 sts	21 sts	23 sts
On Needle 2	9 sts	11 sts	12 sts
On Needle 3	8 sts	10 sts	11 sts
Continue in pattern from chart, shaping top of hand as follows:			
Next Round (decrease round)			
On Needle 1: Ssk with CB, work in pattern to last 2 stitches, K2tog with CB.			
On Needle 2: Ssk with CB, work in pattern to end.			
On Needle 3: Work in pattern to last 2 stitches, K2tog with CB.			
You now have	30 sts	38 sts	42 sts
Next Rounds Repeat the decrease round	6 more times	8 more times	9 more times
To end chart pattern with	Round 14	Round 18	Round 20
You now have	6 sts	6 sts	6 sts

Cut yarn leaving a 10" (25.5 cm) tail of CB. Thread tail on tapestry needle and run through all stitches like a drawstring. Pull tail firmly to close top of hand, and weave in tail on wrong side.

KNITTING THE THUMB	CHILD'S LARGE/ WOMAN'S SMALL	WOMAN'S LARGE	MAN'S LARGE
Place held stitches from thumb gusset on 2 larger double-pointed needles. Join CB and CB to beginning of thumb stitches with right side facing. Knit across thumb stitches in their matching colors, then, using the next color in the 1-stitch stripe sequence, pick up and knit 1 stitch from base of hole where hand stitches rejoined for working in the round. *You now have*	14 sts	16 sts	18 sts
Divide stitches as evenly as possible on three needles.			
Continue in established stripe pattern, working all stitches in their matching colors, until thumb measures	1¾" (2 cm)	2" (5 cm)	2½" (6.5 cm)
Next Round Using CA, *K2tog; repeat from * to end. *You now have*	7 sts	8 sts	9 sts
Cut yarn leaving a 10" (25.5 cm) tail of CA. Thread tail on tapestry needle and run through all stitches like a drawstring. Pull tail firmly to close top of thumb, and weave in tail on wrong side.			

FINISHING

Weave in ends. Use the yarn tail at base of thumb to close up any remaining hole where the thumb meets the hand.

EMBROIDERY

Using a double strand of CC, embroider a line of French knots (see page 197) with about 2 stitches between each pair of knots along the first round of Seed Stitch as shown. Carry the embroidery yarns loosely on the wrong side of the mitten between each pair of French knots so the embroidered section has the same amount of stretch as the rest of the mitten cuff.

Work a second line of French knots in the same manner along the top round of Seed Stitch, aligning the knots directly above the knots in the first line as shown.

French knots along the top and bottom rounds of the Seed Stitch cuff.

■ CA COLEUS
□ CB SPRING GREEN

CHILD'S LARGE/WOMAN'S SMALL

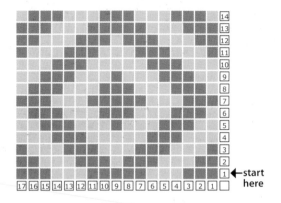

WOMAN'S LARGE

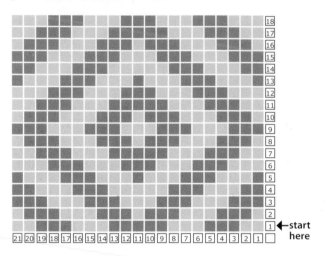

MAN'S LARGE

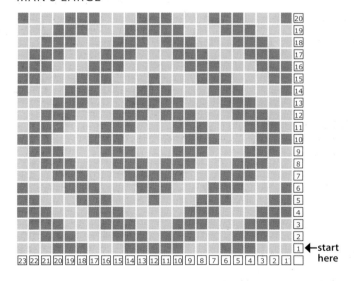

put-it-all-together gloves

It took me years before I decided to knit a pair of gloves. I was always intimidated by the thought of knitting those little fingers. Finally, I decided to put aside my fears and attempt a pair. Needless to say, my fear (as is true of many fears) was not warranted. Knitting fingers, I quickly discovered, is no different from knitting a thumb on a mitten — small and quick. It's just that there are five of them! This pair of gloves has the same diamond motif as used for the Nordic-Inspired Mittens (page 125). After knitting the Fair Isle section in red and chocolate, I worked orange and chartreuse duplicate stitch to put these gloves "over the top."

Plan of action: You start off with stockinette stitch to create a decorative rolled edge and then use Corrugated Rib for the rest of the cuff. You then follow the chart for the diamond pattern on the hands, setting it off on either side by Reverse Stockinette Ridges. (See pages 191 and 195 for instructions on following a chart.) After you finish knitting, work duplicate stitch to enhance the diamonds. Both right and left gloves are knitted exactly the same and can be worn on either hand.

stitches

CORRUGATED RIB
Set Up Round *K2 with CB, K2 with CC; repeat from * to end.
All Other Rounds *K2 with CB, bring CC to front of work, P2 with CC, bring CC to back of work; repeat from * to end.
Repeat the last round only for pattern; do not repeat the Set Up Round.

REVERSE STOCKINETTE RIDGE
Round 1 Knit.
Rounds 2 and 3 Purl.

STOCKINETTE STITCH
Knit all stitches every round.

YARN

Nashua Handknits Julia, 50% wool/25% mohair/25% alpaca, 93 yd (85 m)/1¾ oz (50 g). Yarn band gauge: 5 stitches and 6 rows = 1" (2.5 cm) in Stockinette Stitch on US 7 (4.5 mm) needles.

CA = 2250 French Pumpkin, 1 skein for all sizes
CB = 3961 Ladies Mantle, 1 skein for all sizes
CC = 8118 Espresso, 1 skein for sizes Child's large/Woman's small and Woman's large; 2 skeins for Man's large
CD = 6085 Geranium, 1 skein for all sizes

SIZES AND FINISHED HAND CIRCUMFERENCES

Child's large/Woman's small, 6¾" (17 cm); Woman's large, 8½" (21.5 cm); Man's large, 9¼" (23.5 cm)

Model shown in woman's large.

GAUGE

20 stitches and 21 rounds = 4" (10 cm) in Stockinette Stitch colorwork pattern from chart worked in the round using larger needles.

NEEDLES

Set of four US 7 (4.5 mm) double-pointed needles *or size you need to obtain the correct gauge*

Set of four US 6 (4 mm) double-pointed needles

NOTIONS

Tapestry needle
Stitch markers
Stitch holders

ABBREVIATIONS

K2tog = knit 2 stitches together
M1 = make 1 (see page 200)

KNITTING THE CUFF	CHILD'S LARGE/ WOMAN'S SMALL	WOMAN'S LARGE	MAN'S LARGE
Set Up Using CA and smaller needles cast on	36 sts	40 sts	44 sts
Divide stitches as evenly as possible on three needles. Place marker and join for working in the round, being careful not to twist stitches.			
Next 6 Rounds Work in Stockinette Stitch. The fabric will curl to create a decorative rolled edge at bottom of cuff.			
Next Rounds Change to CB and CC. Work in Corrugated Rib until piece measures from beginning of rib pattern (not including rolled edge)	2" (5 cm)	2½" (6.5 cm)	2½" (6.5 cm)
Next 3 Rounds Change to CA and work 1 Reverse Stockinette Stitch Ridge, and in first round	decrease 2 sts	increase 2 sts	increase 2 sts
You now have	34 sts	42 sts	46 sts
KNITTING THE HAND			
Change to larger needles. **Note** One pattern repeat of the Put-It-All-Together Gloves Chart contains	17 sts	21 sts	23 sts
Using CC and CD as shown, repeat the Put-It-All-Together Gloves Chart for your size 2 times for each round.			
Next Rounds Work in pattern from Put-It-All-Together Gloves Chart for your size until glove measures from beginning of rib pattern (not including rolled edge)	3½" (9 cm)	4" (10 cm)	4½" (11.5 cm)
Next Round			
Work in pattern	17 sts	21 sts	23 sts
Place marker for thumb gusset. M1 (see page 200) using CC. Place marker for thumb gusset.			
Work in pattern	17 sts	21 sts	23 sts
You now have	35 sts	43 sts	47 sts
You now have 1 stitch between the gusset markers for all sizes.			
Next Round Work 1 round even in pattern, working increased stitch using its matching color.			
Next Round (increase round) Work in pattern to first thumb gusset marker, slip marker, M1 using CD, knit to second thumb gusset marker, M1 using CD, slip marker, work in pattern to end: 2 stitches increased between gusset markers.			
Next Round Work 1 round even in pattern, working all thumb gusset stitches in the colors as they appear.			
Next Round (increase round) Work in pattern to first thumb gusset marker, slip marker, M1 using CC, knit to second thumb gusset marker, M1 using CC, slip marker, work in pattern to end: 2 stitches increased between gusset markers.			

KNITTING THE HAND (CONT'D)	CHILD'S LARGE/ WOMAN'S SMALL	WOMAN'S LARGE	MAN'S LARGE
Next Round Work 1 round even in pattern, working all thumb gusset stitches in the colors as they appear.			
Next Rounds Repeat the last 4 rounds	2 more times	2 more times	3 more times
You now have	47 sts	55 sts	63 sts
You now have between the gusset markers	13 sts	13 sts	17 sts

For Woman's large only:

Work 2 more rounds as follows:

	CHILD'S LARGE/ WOMAN'S SMALL	WOMAN'S LARGE	MAN'S LARGE
Next Round (increase round) Work in pattern to first thumb gusset marker, slip marker, M1 using CD, knit to second thumb gusset marker, M1 using CD, work in pattern to end: 2 stitches increased between gusset markers.			
Next Round Work 1 round even in pattern, working all thumb gusset stitches in the colors as they appear. *You now have*	47 sts	57 sts	63 sts
You now have between the gusset markers	13 sts	15 sts	17 sts
Next Round Work in pattern to first gusset marker, remove marker, place gusset stitches on holder, remove second gusset marker, work in pattern to end.			
You now have	34 sts	42 sts	46 sts
Next Rounds Work even in pattern from chart for your size until glove reaches to base of fingers, or measures from beginning of rib pattern (not including rolled edge) about	7" (18 cm)	7½" (19 cm)	8" (20.5 cm)

Make a note of what pattern round you end with so you can make the second glove to match.

Next 3 Rounds Change to smaller needles and CB. Work 1 Reverse Stockinette Ridge.

Place all stitches on a holder.

KNITTING THE THUMB

	CHILD'S LARGE/ WOMAN'S SMALL	WOMAN'S LARGE	MAN'S LARGE
Place held stitches from thumb gusset on 2 smaller double-pointed needles. Join CB to beginning of thumb stitches with right side facing.			
Next Round Knit across thumb stitches, then pick up and knit 1 stitch from base of hole where hand stitches rejoined for working in the round.			
You now have	14 sts	16 sts	18 sts

Divide stitches as evenly as possible on three needles.

Next 2 Rounds Purl with CB to complete Reverse Stockinette Ridge.

KNITTING THE THUMB (CONT'D)	CHILD'S LARGE/ WOMAN'S SMALL	WOMAN'S LARGE	MAN'S LARGE
Next Rounds Change to CD. Work in Stockinette Stitch until thumb measures	1¾" (2 cm)	2" (5 cm)	2½" (6.5 cm)
Next Round Using CD, *K2tog; repeat from * to end.			
You now have	7 sts	8 sts	9 sts

Cut yarn leaving a 10" (25.5 cm) tail of CD. Thread tail on tapestry needle and run through all stitches like a drawstring. Pull tail firmly to close top of thumb, and weave in tail on wrong side.

KNITTING THE FINGERS

The fingers are worked using CD and smaller needles. Leave a 10" (25.5 cm) tail at the beginning of each finger to use later for closing up the holes between fingers.

Pinky

Set Up The pinky edge of the hand is at the beginning of the original hand rounds.

	CHILD'S LARGE/ WOMAN'S SMALL	WOMAN'S LARGE	MAN'S LARGE
From each side of beginning of hand round, place on two separate double-pointed needles	4 sts	5 sts	5 sts
Leave remaining hand stitches on holder.			
You now have	8 sts	10 sts	10 sts

Note The original beginning of the hand round is in the center of these stitches.

Join CD to beginning of pinky stitches with right side facing.

	CHILD'S LARGE/ WOMAN'S SMALL	WOMAN'S LARGE	MAN'S LARGE
Next Round Knit across pinky stitches, then cast on	1 st	1 st	2 sts
You now have	9 sts	11 sts	12 sts

Divide stitches as evenly as possible on three needles.

	CHILD'S LARGE/ WOMAN'S SMALL	WOMAN'S LARGE	MAN'S LARGE
Next Rounds Work in Stockinette Stitch to top of pinky, or until finger measures	2" (5 cm)	2¼" (5.5 cm)	2¾" (7 cm)

Next Round

Child's large/Woman's small only: *K2tog; repeat from * to last stitch, K1.

Woman's large only: *K2tog; repeat from * to last stitch, K1.

Man's large only: *K2tog repeat from * to end.

	CHILD'S LARGE/ WOMAN'S SMALL	WOMAN'S LARGE	MAN'S LARGE
You now have	5 sts	6 sts	6 sts

Cut yarn leaving a 10" (25.5 cm) tail. Thread tail on tapestry needle and run through all stitches like a drawstring. Pull tail firmly to close top of pinky, and weave in tail on wrong side.

KNITTING THE FINGERS (CONT'D)	CHILD'S LARGE/ WOMAN'S SMALL	WOMAN'S LARGE	MAN'S LARGE
Note For the remaining fingers, temporarily decide which side of the hand is the palm side and mark it with a piece of scrap yarn of or safety pin. The finished gloves can be worn on either hand, but you will need to distinguish between the two sides of hand when transferring finger stitches to the needle from the holder, in order to distribute the finger stitches correctly.			
Ring Finger			
Set Up Place on a double-pointed needle from palm side of hand the next	5 sts	5 sts	6 sts
Place on a second double-pointed needle from back of hand the next	4 sts	6 sts	6 sts
You now have	9 sts	11 sts	12 sts
Join CD to beginning of back of hand needle with right side facing.			
Next Round			
Knit across stitches on back of hand needle.			
Pick up and knit from base of pinky	1 st	1 st	2 sts
Knit across stitches from palm needle			
Cast on	1 st	1 st	2 sts
You now have	11 sts	13 sts	16 sts
Divide stitches as evenly as possible on three needles.			
Next Rounds Work in Stockinette Stitch to top of ring finger, or until finger measures	2½" (6.5 cm)	2¾" (7 cm)	3¼" (8.5 cm)
Next Round			
Child's large/Woman's small only: *K2tog; repeat from * to last stitch, K1.			
Woman's large only: *K2tog; repeat from * to last stitch, K1.			
Man's large only: *K2tog repeat from * to end.			
You now have	6 sts	7 sts	8 sts
Complete as for pinky.			
Middle Finger			
Set Up Place on a double-pointed needle from palm side of hand the next	4 sts	6 sts	6 sts
Place on a second double-pointed needle from back of hand the next	5 sts	5 sts	6 sts
You now have	9 sts	11 sts	12 sts
Join CD to beginning of back of hand needle with right side facing.			
Next Round			
Knit across stitches on back of hand needle.			

KNITTING THE FINGERS (CONT'D)	CHILD'S LARGE/ WOMAN'S SMALL	WOMAN'S LARGE	MAN'S LARGE
Pick up and knit from base of ring finger	1 st	1 st	2 sts
Knit across stitches from palm needle.			
Cast on	1 st	1 st	2 sts
You now have	11 sts	13 sts	16 sts
Divide stitches as evenly as possible on three needles.			
Next Rounds Work in Stockinette Stitch to top of middle finger, or until finger measures	2¾" (7 cm)	3" (7.5 cm)	3½" (9 cm)
Next Round			
Child's large/Woman's small only: *K2tog; repeat from * to last stitch, K1.			
Woman's large only: *K2tog; repeat from * to last stitch, K1.			
Man's large only: *K2tog repeat from * to end.			
You now have	6 sts	7 sts	8 sts
Complete as for pinky.			

Index Finger

	CHILD'S LARGE/ WOMAN'S SMALL	WOMAN'S LARGE	MAN'S LARGE
Set Up Divide remaining hand stitches evenly on two separate double-pointed needles.			
You now have	8 sts	10 sts	12 sts
Join CD to beginning of back of palm needle with right side facing.			
Next Round Knit across all index finger stitches, pick up and knit 2 stitches from base of middle finger.			
You now have	10 sts	12 sts	14 sts
Divide stitches as evenly as possible on three needles.			
Next Rounds Work in Stockinette Stitch to top of index finger, or until finger measures	2½" (6.5 cm)	2¾" (7 cm)	3¼" (8.5 cm)
Next Round *K2tog; repeat from * to end.			
You now have	5 sts	6 sts	7 sts
Complete as for pinky.			

FINISHING

Weave in ends. Use the yarn tails at base of thumb and fingers to close up any remaining holes.

EMBROIDERY

Using a single strand of CA, work duplicate stitch embroidery (see page 194) to outline both edges of the inner CD diamond as shown on embroidery chart for your size.

Using a single strand of CB, work duplicate stitch to outline the diagonal lines of CD across each corner of pattern as shown on chart.

Using a single strand of CB, work duplicate stitch to fill in the small center diamond as shown on chart.

Alternating colored duplicate stitches outline small and large diamonds on hand.

PUT-IT-ALL-TOGETHER GLOVES CHARTS

KNITTING YARN COLORS

- ■ CC ESPRESSO
- ■ CD GERANIUM

EMBROIDERY YARN COLORS

- ■ CA FRENCH PUMPKIN
- ■ CB LADIES MANTLE

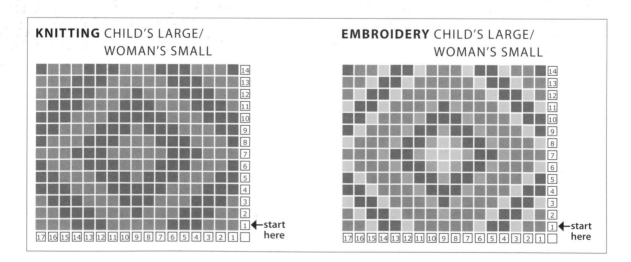

KNITTING CHILD'S LARGE/ WOMAN'S SMALL

EMBROIDERY CHILD'S LARGE/ WOMAN'S SMALL

KNITTING WOMAN'S LARGE

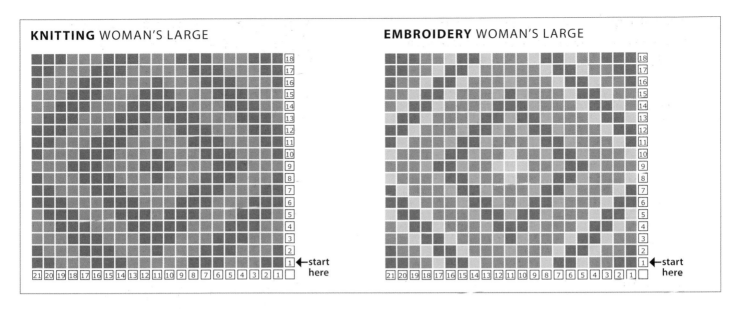

EMBROIDERY WOMAN'S LARGE

KNITTING MAN'S LARGE

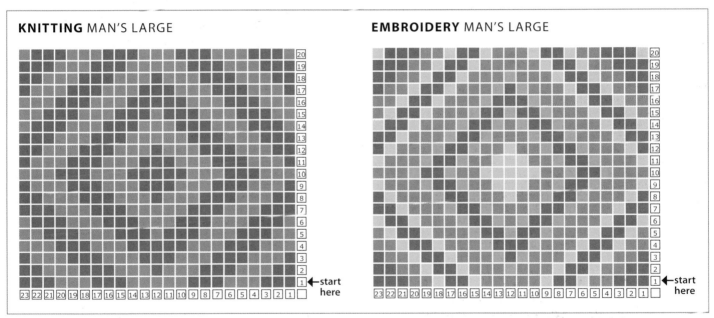

EMBROIDERY MAN'S LARGE

stunning
SWEATERS

ode to picasso

ever since I saw a photo of Picasso wearing a French, striped sailor shirt, I've been enamoured by little stripes. It's 50 years later, but their classic, but chic, look still makes me want to wear mini-stripes. Call these sweaters my "Ode to Picasso," or just a great basic sweater, perfect for you and your daughter or granddaughter. Or, eliminate the embroidered daisies and your little boy will love it too! And I can guarantee, it will still be worn by the next generation.

Plan of action: The back, front and sleeves of the sweater are each knit separately on straight needles and then sewn together. Next the neckband is knit on a circular needle and finally (for the child's version) the embroidered flowers are added. Picking the right colors is the key: Make your stripes stand out by choosing two shades that differ in value (darkness and lightness). (For more about value, see page 12.)

stitches

> **GARTER STITCH**
> Knit all stitches every row.
>
> **GARTER STITCH STRIPES**
> **Rows 1 and 2** Knit with CB.
> **Rows 3 and 4** Knit with CA.
> Repeat Rows 1–4 for pattern.
> **Note** Rows 1 and 3 are right side rows; Rows 2 and 4 are wrong side rows.
>
> **K2, P2 RIB**
> Work all rounds as *K2, P2; repeat from * to end of round.

YARN

Nashua Handknits Julia, 50% wool/ 25% mohair/25% alpaca, 93 yd (85 m)/ 1¾ oz (50 g). Yarn band gauge: 5 stitches and 6 rows = 1" (2.5 cm) in Stockinette Stitch on US 7 (4.5 mm) needles.

Child's version:
CA = 6416 Midnight Blue, 3 skeins for Small and Medium; 4 skeins for Large and Extra-large
CB = 8141 Pretty Pink, 5 skeins for Small and Medium; 6 skeins for Large; 7 skeins for Extra-large

Adult's version:
CA = 6396 Deep Blue Sea, 5 skeins for Small and Medium; 6 skeins for Large and Extra-large
CB = 3961 Ladies Mantle, 12 skeins for Small; 13 skeins for Medium; 14 skeins for Large; 15 skeins for Extra-large

SIZES AND FINISHED CHEST MEASUREMENTS

Child: Small 26½" (67.5 cm), Medium 28½" (72.5 cm), Large 30" (76 cm), Extra-large 32" (81.5 cm). Model shown is size large.

Adult: Small 38" (96.5 cm), Medium 42" (106.5 cm), Large 45" (114.5 cm), Extra-large 49" (124.5 cm). Model shown is size medium.

GAUGE

18 stitches and 32 rows = 4" (10 cm) in Garter Stitch.

NEEDLES

US 8 (5 mm) straight needles *or size you need to obtain the correct gauge*

US 7 (4.5 mm) circular needles 16" (40 cm) long for neckband

NOTIONS

Tapestry needle

Stitch marker

Removable markers or safety pins (for marking sleeve positions)

CHILD'S PULLOVER	SMALL	MEDIUM	LARGE	EXTRA-LARGE
KNITTING THE BACK				
Set Up With CA and straight needles, cast on	60 sts	64 sts	68 sts	72 sts
Next Row With CA, knit.				
Next Rows Change to CB. Changing colors as indicated for pattern, work in Garter Stitch Stripes, until piece measures from cast-on edge End having just completed Row 4 of Garter Stitch Stripes pattern.	10½" (26.5cm)	11" (28 cm)	11½" (29 cm)	12" (30.5 cm)
Next Rows Change to CB. Work in Garter Stitch using only CB until piece measures from cast-on edge	15" (38 cm)	16" (40.5 cm)	17" (43 cm)	18" (45.5 cm)
Bind off all stitches.				
KNITTING THE FRONT				
Work as for back, ending with a wrong side row, until piece measures from cast-on edge	13½" (34.5 cm)	14½" (37 cm)	15½" (39.5 cm)	16½" (42 cm)
Front Neck				
With right side facing you, knit across first	23 sts	25 sts	26 sts	27 sts
Join a second ball of CB and bind off center	14 sts	14 sts	16 sts	18 sts
Knit across remaining	23 sts	25 sts	26 sts	27 sts
You now have two groups of	23 sts	25 sts	26 sts	27 sts
Next Row (wrong side) Knit across the first group of stitches, bind off 1 stitch at beginning of next group of stitches (neck edge), knit to end.				
Next Row (right side) Knit across the first group of stitches, bind off 1 stitch at beginning of next group of stitches (neck edge), knit to end. *You now have* two groups of	22 sts	24 sts	25 sts	26 sts
Repeat the last 2 rows 3 more times. *You now have* two groups of	19 sts	21 sts	22 sts	23 sts
Working each side separately, work even in Garter Stitch until piece measures from cast-on edge	15" (38 cm)	16" (40.5 cm)	17" (43 cm)	18" (45.5 cm)
Bind off all stitches.				
KNITTING THE SLEEVES				
Set Up With CB and straight needles, cast on	30 sts	34 sts	36 sts	38 sts
Next Rows Work in Garter Stitch using only CB until piece measures 3½" (9 cm) from cast-on edge.				

KNITTING THE SLEEVES (CONT'D)	SMALL	MEDIUM	LARGE	EXTRA LARGE
Next Rows Continue in Garter Stitch, and increase 1 stitch at each end of needle every 8th row	5 times	5 times	6 times	7 times
You now have	40 sts	44 sts	48 sts	52 sts
Next Rows Work even in Garter Stitch until piece measures from cast-on edge	10" (25.5 cm)	11" (28 cm)	12" (30.5 cm)	13" (33 cm)
Bind off all stitches.				
FINISHING				
Sew shoulder seams.				
Measure down from each shoulder seam along sides of front and back ___, and place markers	4½" (11.5 cm)	5" (12.5 cm)	5½" (14 cm)	6" (15 cm)
Sew sleeves to body between markers. Sew sleeve and side seams. (See illustration for adult version on page 147.)				
WORKING THE NECKBAND				
Set Up With CB and circular needle, beginning at one shoulder seam pick up and knit around neck opening	64 sts	68 sts	68 sts	72 sts
Place marker and join for working in the round.				
Next Rounds Work in K2, P2 Rib until neckband measures 2" (5 cm). Bind off all stitches loosely.				
Weave in ends. Steam or block to finished measurements, if desired (see page 204).				

EMBROIDERY

Using a single strand of CA, embroider six five-petaled flowers using lazy daisy stitch (see page 197) on front yoke of sweater as shown. With single strand of CA, embroider a French knot (see page 197) in the center of each flower as shown.

Lazy daisy worked on garter-stitch background.

ADULT'S PULLOVER	SMALL	MEDIUM	LARGE	EXTRA-LARGE
KNITTING THE BACK				
Set Up With CA and straight needles, cast on	85 sts	94 sts	102 sts	110 sts
Next Row With CA, knit.				
Next Rows Change to CB. Changing colors as indicated for pattern, work in Garter Stitch Stripes, until piece measures 16½" (42 cm) from cast-on edge for all sizes, and end having just completed Row 4 of Garter Stitch Stripes pattern.				
Next Rows Change to CB. Work in Garter Stitch using only CB until piece measures from cast-on edge	25" (63.5 cm)	25½" (65 cm)	26" (66 cm)	26½" (67.5 cm)
Bind off all stitches.				
KNITTING THE FRONT				
Work as for back, ending with a wrong side row, until piece measures from cast-on edge	23" (58.5 cm)	23½" (59.5 cm)	24" (61 cm)	24½" (62 cm)
Front Neck				
With right side facing you, knit across first	34 sts	38 sts	40 sts	44 sts
Join a second ball of CB and bind off center	17 sts	18 sts	22 sts	22 sts
Knit across remaining	34 sts	38 sts	40 sts	44 sts
You now have two groups of	34 sts	38 sts	40 sts	44 sts
Next Row (wrong side) Knit across the first group of stitches, bind off 1 stitch at beginning of next group of stitches (neck edge), knit to end.				
Next Row (right side) Knit across the first group of stitches, bind off 1 stitch at beginning of next group of stitches (neck edge), knit to end. *You now have* two groups of	33 sts	37 sts	39 sts	43 sts
Repeat the last 2 rows 3 more times. *You now have* two groups of	30 sts	34 sts	36 sts	40 sts
Working each side separately, work even in Garter Stitch until piece measures from cast-on edge	25" (63.5 cm)	25½" (65 cm)	26" (66 cm)	26½" (67.5 cm)
Bind off all stitches.				
KNITTING THE SLEEVES				
Set Up With CB and straight needles, cast on	42 sts	46 sts	50 sts	52 sts
Next Rows Work in Garter Stitch using only CB until piece measures 4" (10.5 cm) from cast-on edge.				

KNITTING THE SLEEVES (CONT'D)	SMALL	MEDIUM	LARGE	EXTRA LARGE
Next Rows Continue in Garter Stitch, and increase 1 stitch at each end of needle every 6th row	17 times	17 times	17 times	18 times
You now have	76 sts	80 sts	84 sts	88 sts
Next Rows Work even in Garter Stitch, if necessary, until piece measures from cast-on edge 17¾" (45 cm) for all sizes.				
Bind off all stitches.				

FINISHING

Sew shoulder seams. (See page 204.)				
Measure down from each shoulder seam along sides of front and back ___ , and place markers	8½" (21.5 cm)	9" (23 cm)	9½" (24 cm)	10" (25.5 cm)
Sew sleeves to body between markers. Sew sleeve and side seams. (See illustration below.)				

WORKING THE NECKBAND

Set Up With CB and circular needle, beginning at one shoulder seam pick up and knit around neck opening	68 sts	72 sts	76 sts	76 sts
Place marker and join for working in the round.				
Next Rounds Work in K2, P2 Rib until neckband measures 5" (12.5 cm). Bind off all stitches loosely.				
Weave in ends. Steam or block to finished measurements, if desired (see page 203).				

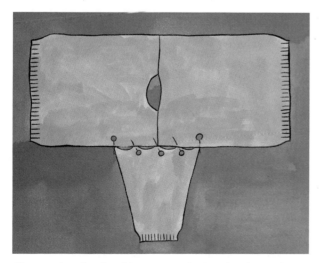

After sewing the shoulder seams, pinning the sleeves into the body, in preparation for stitching them in place.

circles, bobbles, and stripes

Combining stripes and circles in one garment gives an Op-Art look to this pull-over. A neckline trimmed with pom poms and a bobbled edging further adds to the colorful circle theme.

Plan of action: The body of the sweater is worked in the round to the beginning of the armholes, then divided for working the back and front separately back and forth in rows. The sleeves are worked separately in the round and sewn into the armhole during finishing. See pages 191 and 195 for instructions on working from a chart.

YARN

Nashua Handknits Julia, 50% wool/25% mohair/25% alpaca, 93 yd (85 m)/1¾ oz (50 g). Yarn band gauge: 5 stitches and 6 rows = 1" (2.5 cm) in Stockinette Stitch on US 7 (4.5 mm) needles.

CA = 2083 Magenta, 5 skeins for Extra-small; 6 skeins for Small and Medium; 7 skeins for Large

CB = 2163 Golden Honey, 2 skeins for Extra-small and Small; 3 skeins for Medium and Large

CC = 6085 Geranium, 5 skeins for Extra-small; 6 skeins for Small and Medium; 7 skeins for Large

CD = 4936 Blue Thyme, 2 skeins for Extra-small, Small, and Medium; 3 skeins for Large

CE = 8118, Espresso, 1 skein for all sizes

stitches

BOBBLE EDGING
*P9, (K1, YO, K1, YO, K1) all in same stitch to increase 1 stitch to 5 stitches, turn work so wrong side is facing, K5 bobble stitches, turn work so right side is facing, P5 bobble stitches, pass second, third, fourth, and fifth stitches on right needle over first stitch to decrease bobble back to 1 st; repeat from * to end of round.

K3, P3 RIB
Work all rounds as *K3, P3; repeat from * to end of round.

REVERSE STOCKINETTE RIDGE
Round 1 Knit.
Rounds 2 and 3 Purl.

STOCKINETTE STITCH IN ROWS
Knit all stitches on right side rows, and purl all stitches on wrong side rows.

STOCKINETTE STITCH IN THE ROUND
Knit all stitches every round.

STRIPE PATTERN
Rows/Rounds 1 and 2 Work in Stockinette Stitch using CC.
Rows/Rounds 3 and 4 Work in Stockinette Stitch using CA.
Repeat these 4 rows or rounds for stripe pattern.

SIZES AND FINISHED CHEST MEASUREMENTS
Extra-small 36¾" (93.5 cm), Small 41" (104 cm), Medium 45½" (115.5 cm), Large 49¾" (126.5 cm). Model shown is size small.

GAUGE
Note You will need 3 gauge swatches: (1) Stockinette Stitch in the Round, (2) Stockinette Stitch in Rows, and (3) in the round in Fair Isle pattern stitch.

19 stitches and 24 rows/rounds = 4" (10 cm) striped Stockinette Stitch.

21 stitches and 21½ rounds = 4" (10 cm) in Stockinette Stitch colorwork pattern from charts worked in the round.

NEEDLES
US 8 (5 mm) circular needles 16" (40 cm) and 24" or 29" (60 or 75 cm) long *or size you need to obtain the correct gauge*

Set of four or five US 8 (5 mm) double-pointed needles *or size you need to obtain the correct gauge*

NOTIONS
Tapestry needle

Stitch holder or scrap yarn

Stitch marker

US G/6 (4 mm) crochet hook

Pompom maker (optional) or scrap cardboard

ABBREVIATIONS
K2tog = knit 2 stitches together
YO = Yarnover

KNITTING THE LOWER BODY	EXTRA-SMALL	SMALL	MEDIUM	LARGE
Set Up With CA and longer circular needle, cast on	170 sts	190 sts	210 sts	230 sts
Place marker and join for working in the round, being careful not to twist stitches.				
Round 1 Work Bobble Edging.				
Round 2 Knit.				
Round 3 Purl.				
Rounds 4–6 Change to CB and work 1 Reverse Stockinette Ridge.				
Rounds 7–9 Change to CC and work 1 Reverse Stockinette Ridge.				
Rounds 10–12 Change to CD and work 1 Reverse Stockinette Ridge.				
Rounds 13–15 Change to CE and work 1 Reverse Stockinette Ridge.				
Rounds 16 and 17 Change to CB and knit 2 rounds.				
Round 18 Knit with CB, increasing evenly	19 sts	20 sts	21 sts	22 sts
You now have	189 sts	210 sts	231 sts	252 sts
Rounds 19–38 Using CB and CD as shown, work Rounds 1–20 of Large Circle Chart.				
Round 39 Knit with CB, decreasing evenly	19 sts	20 sts	21 sts	22 sts
You now have	170 sts	190 sts	210 sts	230 sts
Rounds 40 and 41 With CB, knit 2 rounds.				
Rounds 42–44 Change to CE and work 1 Reverse Stockinette Ridge. Piece measures about 6½" (16.5 cm) from cast-on edge.				
Next Rounds Change to CC and CA. Work even in Stripe Pattern until piece measures from cast-on edge	13" (33 cm)	13½" (34.5 cm)	14" (35.5 cm)	14½" (37 cm)
End having just finished a complete 2-round stripe.				
Dividing Round Using the next color required by Stripe Pattern, divide stitches for back and front as follows:				
For back, knit	85 sts	95 sts	105 sts	115 sts
Place on holder for front the next	85 sts	95 sts	105 sts	115 sts
You now have on needle for back	85 sts	95 sts	105 sts	115 sts

KNITTING THE BACK	EXTRA-SMALL	SMALL	MEDIUM	LARGE
Continue working established Stripe Pattern back and forth in Stockinette Stitch in Rows until piece measures from cast-on edge	21" (53.5 cm)	22" (56 cm)	23" (58.5 cm)	24" (61 cm)
Armhole measures from dividing round about	8" (20.5 cm)	8½" (21.5 cm)	9" (23 cm)	9½" (24 cm)

End having just completed a 2-row stripe.

Bind off all stitches.

KNITTING THE FRONT

Return held front stitches to longer circular needle and join yarn with right side facing.

	EXTRA-SMALL	SMALL	MEDIUM	LARGE
You now have	85 sts	95 sts	105 sts	115 sts
Continue working established Stripe Pattern back and forth in Stockinette Stitch in Rows until piece measures from cast-on edge	18½" (47 cm)	19½" (49.5 cm)	20½" (52 cm)	21½" (54.5 cm)

End having just finished a wrong side row.

SHAPE FRONT NECK

	EXTRA-SMALL	SMALL	MEDIUM	LARGE
Continuing established Stripe Pattern, with right side facing you, knit across first	36 sts	40 sts	44 sts	49 sts
Join a second ball of yarn and bind off center	13 sts	15 sts	17 sts	17 sts
Knit across remaining	36 sts	40 sts	44 sts	49 sts
You now have two groups of	36 sts	40 sts	44 sts	49 sts

Next Row (wrong side) Purl across the first group of stitches, bind off 2 stitches at beginning of next group of stitches (neck edge), purl to end.

Next Row (right side) Knit across the first group of stitches, bind off 2 stitches at beginning of next group of stitches (neck edge), knit to end.

	EXTRA-SMALL	SMALL	MEDIUM	LARGE
You now have two groups of	34 sts	38 sts	42 sts	47 sts
Repeat the last 2 rows 3 more times. *You now have* two groups of	28 sts	32 sts	36 sts	41 sts
Working each side separately, work even in Stripe Pattern until piece measures from cast-on edge	21" (53.5 cm)	22" (56 cm)	23" (58.5 cm)	24" (61 cm)
Armhole measures from dividing round about	8" (20.5 cm)	8½" (21.5 cm)	9" (23 cm)	9½" (24 cm)

End having just completed a 2-row stripe with the same color as the last stripe on the back.

Bind off all stitches.

KNITTING THE SLEEVES	EXTRA-SMALL	SMALL	MEDIUM	LARGE
Note When increasing for the sleeves, change to shorter circular needle when there are too many stitches to fit comfortably around the double-pointed needles.				
Set Up With CA and double-pointed needles, cast on 50 stitches for all sizes. Divide stitches as evenly as possible on three needles, place marker, and join for working in the round, being careful not to twist stitches.				
Round 1 Work Bobble Edging.				
Round 2 Knit.				
Round 3 Purl.				
Rounds 4–6 Change to CB and work 1 Reverse Stockinette Ridge.				
Rounds 7–9 Change to CC and work 1 Reverse Stockinette Ridge.				
Rounds 10–12 Change to CD and work 1 Reverse Stockinette Ridge.				
Rounds 13–15 Change to CE and work 1 Reverse Stockinette Ridge.				
Rounds 16–18 Change to CB and knit 3 rounds.				
Rounds 19–26 Using CB and CD as shown, work Rounds 1–8 of Small Circle Chart.				
Rounds 27–29 With CB, knit 3 rounds.				
Rounds 30–32 Change to CE and work 1 Reverse Stockinette Ridge. Piece measures about 4¼" (11 cm) from cast-on edge.				
Next 2 Rounds Change to CC and work Rounds 1 and 2 of Stripe Pattern.				
Increase Round Continuing in Stripe Pattern, increase 1 stitch at each end of round as follows: K1, M1, knit to last stitch, M1, K1: 2 stitches increased.				
Next Rounds Continuing in established Stripe Pattern, work increase round every 4th round *You now have*	11 more times 74 sts	13 more times 78 sts	16 more times 84 sts	18 more times 88 sts
Next Rounds Continue in established Stripe Pattern until piece measures from cast-on edge	20" (51 cm)	19½" (49.5 cm)	18½" (47 cm)	17½" (44.5 cm)

KNITTING THE SLEEVES (CONT'D)	EXTRA-SMALL	SMALL	MEDIUM	LARGE
End having just completed a 2-round stripe.				
Note Because the larger sizes have increasingly wider bodies, they have shorter sleeves in order to prevent the "wingspan" of the sweater from becoming too wide and the sleeves from becoming too long.				
Bind off all stitches.				

KNITTING THE TURTLENECK

	EXTRA-SMALL	SMALL	MEDIUM	LARGE
Sew shoulder seams.				
Set Up Using CE and shorter circular needle, pick up and knit around neck opening Place marker and join for working in the round.	70 sts	70 sts	70 sts	80 sts
Rounds 1 and 2 Purl.				
Round 3 Knit.				
Round 4 Work eyelet holes for neckline tie as follows: *K1, YO, K2tog, K2; repeat from * to end. *You now have*	14 eyelet holes	14 eyelet holes	14 eyelet holes	18 eyelet holes
Round 5 Knit.				
Round 6 Purl.				
Round 7 Purl, increasing evenly *You now have*	2 sts 72 sts	8 sts 78 sts	8 sts 78 sts	4 sts 84 sts
Next Rounds Change to CD. Work in K3, P3 Rib until rib pattern measures 4" (10 cm), or desired length.				
Bind off all stitches loosely in Rib Pattern.				

FINISHING

Sew sleeves into armholes. Weave in ends.

EMBROIDERY

Using a single strand of either CA or CC, work chain stitch embroidery (see page 197) around the outside of every other knitted circle motif as shown, working in a smooth line to round the outline of the circle.

Using a single strand of either CA or CC, but working with the opposite color from the one you used for the first set of circles, work chain stitch embroidery around the outside edge of the remaining knitted circles as shown.

Using a single strand of either CA or CC, work chain stitch embroidery around the inner edge of each knitted circle, using the opposite color from the one used for the outside of the circle as shown.

TIES

With crochet hook and CD, work a 30" (76 cm) crochet chain. Fasten off last stitch. Weave in ends of tie.

Beginning with the eyelet hole closest to center front, weave the tie in and out of the eyelet holes all the way around the neck.

POMPOMS

Make two pompoms (see page 199) in the colors of your choice. The pompoms shown use the CA, CB, and CD for one pompom, and CB, CC, and CD for the other. Attach pompoms to the ends of ties as shown.

Inner and outer circles outlined by chain stitch.

Crocheted ties woven through eyelets at base of turtleneck, then embellished with pompoms.

CIRCLES, BOBBLES, AND STRIPES CHARTS

LARGE CIRCLE CHART

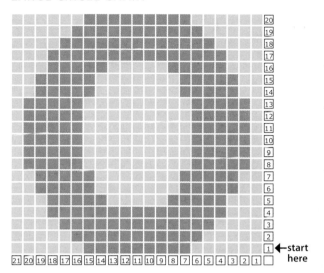

SMALL CIRCLE CHART

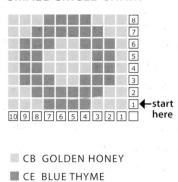

■ CB GOLDEN HONEY
■ CE BLUE THYME

CIRCLES, BOBBLES, AND STRIPES SCHEMATIC

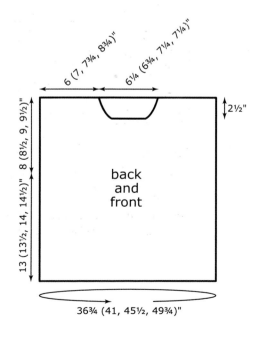

6 (7, 7¾, 8¾)"

6¼ (6¾, 7¼, 7¼)"

2½"

8 (8½, 9, 9½)"

13 (13½, 14, 14½)"

back and front

36¾ (41, 45½, 49¾)"

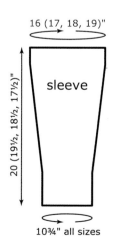

16 (17, 18, 19)"

20 (19½, 18½, 17½)"

sleeve

10¾" all sizes

diamond panes pullover

a horizontal band of boxes edges the diamond design on this challenging turtleneck. Embroidered flowers embellish the pattern field and contrasting edges further enhance this colorful winter pullover.

Plan of action: The body of the sweater is worked in the round to the shoulders with steeked sections for the armholes and front neck. During finishing, the steeks are secured with hand or machine stitching then cut open. The sleeves are worked separately in the round and sewn into cut armhole openings. The picot edging is added to the lower edge of the body and sleeve cuffs during finishing. See pages 191 and 195 for information on working from a chart.

YARN

Nashua Handknits Julia, 50% wool/ 25% mohair/25% alpaca, 93 yd (85 m)/ 1¾ oz (50 g). Yarn band gauge: 5 stitches and 6 rows = 1" (2.5 cm) in Stockinette Stitch on US 7 (4.5 mm) needles.

CA = 2083 Magenta, 1 skein for Small, Medium, and Large; 2 skeins for Extra-large

CB = 3961 Ladies Mantle, 2 skeins for Small, Medium, and Large; 3 skeins for Extra-large

CC = 5178 Lupine, 6 skeins for Small; 7 skeins for Medium; 8 skeins for Large; 9 skeins for Extra-large

CD = 2163 Golden Honey, 2 skeins for Small and Medium; 3 skeins for Large and Extra-large

CE = 0178 Harvest Spice, 1 skein for Small and Medium; 2, skeins for Large and Extra-large

CF = 8118 Espresso, 6 skeins for Small; 7 skeins for Medium; 8 skeins for Large; 9 skeins for Extra-large

stitches

GARTER RIDGE
Round 1 Knit.
Round 2 Purl.

K3, P3 RIB
Work all rounds as *K3, P3; repeat from * to end of round.

PICOT BIND OFF
Turn work so wrong side is facing you. Bind off 3 stitches as if to knit. *Slip the stitch on right needle back to left needle and knit it again, then return the same stitch to left needle and knit it once more: stitch will end up on right needle. Bind off the next 5 stitches as if to knit. Repeat from * until 2 stitches remain, 1 stitch on each needle. Slip the stitch on right needle back to left needle and knit it again, then return the same stitch to left needle and knit it once more. Bind off last 2 stitches.

STOCKINETTE STITCH
Knit all stitches every round.

SIZES AND FINISHED CHEST MEASUREMENTS

Small 38½" (98 cm), Medium 43¼" (110 cm), Large 48" (122 cm), Extra-large 52¾" (134 cm). Model shown is size medium.

GAUGE

20 stitches and 20½ rounds = 4" (10 cm) in Stockinette Stitch colorwork pattern from charts worked in the round using larger needles.

NEEDLES

US 7 (4.5 mm) circular needles 16" (40 cm) and 24" or 29" (60 or 75 cm) long *or size you need to obtain the correct gauge*

US 6 (4 mm) circular needles 16" (40 cm) and 24" or 29" (60 or 75 cm) long

Set of four or five US 7 (4.5 mm) double-pointed needles *or size you need to obtain the correct gauge*

Set of four or five US 6 (4 mm) double-pointed needles

NOTIONS

Tapestry needle

Stitch markers

Sewing machine or sewing needle and matching thread for sewing steeks

ABBREVIATIONS

K2tog = knit 2 stitches together

M1 = make 1 (see page 200)

Ssk = slip, slip, knit these 2 stitches together

KNITTING THE BODY	SMALL	MEDIUM	LARGE	EXTRA-LARGE
Set Up With CA and smaller, longer circular needle, cast on	192 sts	216 sts	240 sts	264 sts
Place marker and join for working in the round, being careful not to twist stitches.				
Next Round Purl.				
Next Round Change to CB and knit 1 round.				
Next Rounds Change to K3, P3 Rib and work until piece measures 2½" (6.5 cm) from beginning of rib pattern.				
Next 2 Rounds Change to CA and work 1 Garter Ridge.				
Next 2 Rounds Change to CC and work 1 Garter Ridge.				
Next 13 Rounds Change to larger, longer circular needle. Using CD and CE as shown, work Rounds 1–13 of Squares Chart once.				
Note If a color is not used for 5 or more stitches in the charted section, twist the unused color together with the working color to catch it against the back of the fabric (see page 192).				
Next 2 Rounds Change to CF and work 1 Garter Ridge.				
Next 2 Rounds Change to CA and work 1 Garter Ridge.				
Piece measures about 5½" (14 cm) from cast-on edge.				
Next Rounds Using CD and CE as shown, repeat Rounds 1–10 of Diamonds Chart until piece measures from cast-on edge	14" (35.5 cm)	14½" (37 cm)	15" (38 cm)	15½" (39.5 cm)
Place a marker in the last round after ____ to mark the halfway point of the round for the side "seam" and steek placement.	96 sts	108 sts	120 sts	132 sts
Next Round Continue in pattern from chart and establish steek stitches as follows:				
Using the backward loop cast-on method (see page 200), cast on 3 stitches before the beginning of the round as follows: 1 stitch CC, 1 stitch CF, 1 stitch CC.				
Place marker.				
Work in pattern from chart to side seam marker and slip marker.				

KNITTING THE BODY (CONT'D)	SMALL	MEDIUM	LARGE	EXTRA-LARGE
Using the backward loop method, cast on 6 stitches as follows: *1 stitch CF, 1 stitch CC; repeat from * two more times, removing side seam marker when you come to it.				
Place marker.				
Work in pattern from chart to end of round.				
Using the backward loop cast-on method cast on 3 stitches at end of the round as follows: 1 stitch CF, 1 stitch CC, 1 stitch CF.				
You now have	204 sts	228 sts	252 sts	276 sts
One group each for front and back with	96 sts	108 sts	120 sts	132 sts
One group of 6 steek stitches on each side of body				
Note Although you have just ended in the middle of a 6-stitch steek group, from here on the new beginning of the round is at the start of that same steek group.				
Next Rounds Working marked groups of 6 steek stitches in pattern from Steeks Chart, continue in established pattern from Diamonds Chart on front and back until piece measures from cast-on edge	19½" (49.5 cm)	20½" (52 cm)	21½" (54.5 cm)	22½" (57 cm)

SHAPE FRONT NECK

	SMALL	MEDIUM	LARGE	EXTRA-LARGE
Next Round Continue in established patterns from charts and shape neck as follows:				
Work 6 steek stitches in pattern.				
Work in Diamonds pattern	36 sts	41 sts	46 sts	52 sts
Using CC bind off center	24 sts	26 sts	28 sts	28 sts
Work in Diamonds pattern	36 sts	41 sts	46 sts	52 sts
Work 6 steek stitches in pattern.				
Work in Diamonds pattern to end.				
You now have on the front on each side of bound-off front neck	36 sts	41 sts	46 sts	52 sts
Next Round Continue in patterns from chart and establish steek stitches for front neck as follows:				
Work 6 steek stitches in pattern.				
Work in Diamonds pattern	36 sts	41 sts	46 sts	52 sts
Place marker.				
Using the backward loop method, cast on 6 stitches as follows: *1 stitch CF, 1 stitch CC; repeat from * two more times				
Place marker.				

SHAPE FRONT NECK (CONT'D)	SMALL	MEDIUM	LARGE	EXTRA-LARGE
Work in Diamonds pattern	36 sts	41 sts	46 sts	52 sts
Work 6 steek stitches in pattern.				
Work in Diamonds pattern to end.				
You now have	186 sts	208 sts	230 sts	254 sts
One group each on each side of front neck with	36 sts	41 sts	46 sts	52 sts
One group of 6 steek stitches at center front				
One group of 6 steek stitches on each side of body				
One group for back with	96 sts	108 sts	120 sts	132 sts

Next Round (decrease round) Work in established patterns to 2 stitches before marked 6-stitch group at center front, K2tog, work center front stitches in pattern from Steeks Chart, ssk, work in established patterns to end: 2 stitches decreased, 1 on either side of center front steek.

Next Round Work 1 round even in established patterns.

	SMALL	MEDIUM	LARGE	EXTRA-LARGE
Repeat the last 2 rounds 3 more times.				
You now have	178 sts	200 sts	222 sts	246 sts
One group each on each side of front neck with	32 sts	37 sts	42 sts	48 sts
One group of 6 steek stitches at center front				
One group of 6 steek stitches on each side of body				
One group for back with	96 sts	108 sts	120 sts	132 sts
Work even in established patterns until piece measures from cast-on edge	22" (56 cm)	23" (58.5 cm)	24" (61 cm)	25" (63.5 cm)
Armhole measures from beginning of side steeks about	8" (20.5 cm)	8½" (21.5 cm)	9" (23 cm)	9½" (24 cm)

Bind off all stitches.

KNITTING THE SLEEVES

	SMALL	MEDIUM	LARGE	EXTRA-LARGE
Note When increasing for the sleeves, change to larger, shorter circular needle when there are too many stitches to fit comfortably around the double-pointed needles.				
Set Up With CA and smaller double-pointed needles, cast on	48 sts	48 sts	48 sts	48 sts
Divide stitches as evenly as possible on three needles, place marker, and join for working in the round, being careful not to twist stitches.				

Next Round Purl.

KNITTING THE SLEEVES (CONT'D)	SMALL	MEDIUM	LARGE	EXTRA-LARGE

Next Rounds Change to CB. Work in K3, P3 Rib until piece measures 3" (7.5 cm) from beginning of rib pattern.

Next 2 Rounds Change to CA and work 1 Garter Ridge.

Next 2 Rounds Change to CE and work 1 Garter Ridge, making two evenly spaced M1 increases (see page 200) in second round of ridge. *You now have*

	SMALL	MEDIUM	LARGE	EXTRA-LARGE
	50 sts	50 sts	50 sts	50 sts

Piece measures about 3¼" (8.5 cm) from cast-on edge.

Next Rounds Change to larger double-pointed needles. Using CC and CF, set up patterns as follows:

K1 with CC.

Place marker.

Work Diamonds pattern from chart over next 48 stitches.

Place marker.

K1 with CF.

Note The first and last stitches of every sleeve round are worked alternating CC and CF as for the steek sections of the body. In other words, every time you work the first or last stitch of the round, work it using the opposite color from the way it appears.

Increase Round Continuing in established patterns, increase 1 stitch at each end of round as follows: Work 1 stitch in alternating color pattern, M1, work in Diamonds pattern to last stitch, M1, work 1 stitch in alternating color pattern: 2 stitches increased.

Next Rounds Continuing in established patterns, and working new stitches into Diamonds pattern from chart, work increase round

	SMALL	MEDIUM	LARGE	EXTRA-LARGE
Every other round	0 times	0 times	7 times	16 times
Then every 4th round	14 times	17 times	12 times	6 times
You now have	80 sts	86 sts	90 sts	96 sts

Next Rounds Continue in established patterns until piece measures from cast-on edge

	SMALL	MEDIUM	LARGE	EXTRA-LARGE
	19½" (49.5 cm)	19" (48.5 cm)	17½" (44.5 cm)	16" (40.5 cm)

Note Because the larger sizes have increasingly wider bodies, they have shorter sleeves in order to prevent the "wingspan" of the sweater from becoming too wide and the sleeves from becoming too long.

KNITTING THE SLEEVES (CONT'D)	SMALL	MEDIUM	LARGE	EXTRA-LARGE
Bind off all stitches.				

SECURING THE STEEKS

Secure the steeks for cutting as shown on page 203. Using sewing machine set to zigzag stitch, stitch down the middle of the stitches on each side of the center of the armhole steeks. Using sewing machine set to straight stitch, sew in the ditch between the Diamonds pattern and Steeks pattern on each side of armhole steeks. Carefully cut the armholes open along the center of the steeks from bound-off edge to beginning of steeks. Secure and cut front neck steek in the same manner.

KNITTING THE TURTLENECK

Sew shoulder seams.

	SMALL	MEDIUM	LARGE	EXTRA-LARGE
Set Up Using CD and larger, shorter circular needle, pick up and knit (see below) around neck opening	72 sts	72 sts	78 sts	78 sts

Place marker and join for working in the round.

Next Round Purl.

Next 2 Rounds Change to CA and work 1 Garter Ridge.

Next Rounds Change to CB. Work in K3, P3 Rib until piece measures 1" (2.5 cm) from beginning of rib pattern.

Next Rounds Change to smaller, shorter circular needle. Continue in K3, P3 Rib with CB until piece measures 3" (7.5 cm) from beginning of rib pattern.

Next 2 Rounds Change to CF and work 1 Garter Ridge.

Next Round Change to CA and knit 1 round.

Using CA, work Picot Bind Off.

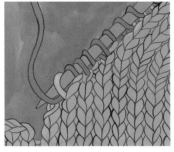

Picking up and knitting stitches along neck edge.

DIAMOND PANES CHARTS

■ CC LUPINE
▢ CD GOLDEN HONEY
■ CE HARVEST SPICE
■ CF ESPRESSO

DIAMONDS CHART

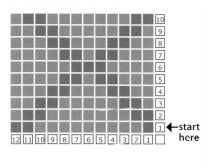

SQUARES CHART

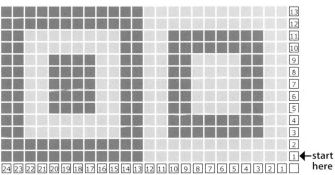

STEEKS CHART

DIAMOND PANES SCHEMATIC

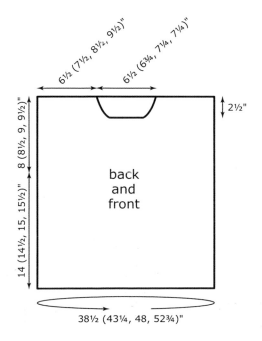

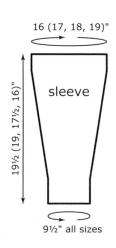

FINISHING

Sew sleeves into armholes. Weave in ends.

PICOT EDGING FOR LOWER BODY & CUFFS

With CA and smaller longer circular needle, with right side of sweater facing you, pick up and knit from cast-on edge of lower body: 190 sts, 215 sts, 240 sts, 265 sts

Using CA, work Picot Bind Off.

With CB and smaller double-pointed needles and right side of sleeve facing you, pick up and knit 50 stitches from cast-on edge of sleeve cuff. Using CB, work Picot Bind Off. Repeat for other sleeve.

EMBROIDERY

Using a single strand of CA, work a row of lazy daisies (see page 197) along the first Round 6 of Diamonds pattern in body, placing each daisy at the point where two diamonds come together as shown.

▶ *For size Medium only,* there are enough stitches so you can begin the daisies at any diamond intersection point in the round and leave 36 stitches between each pair of daisies all the way around.

▶ *For all other sizes,* begin by embroidering a daisy at the point closest to center front where two diamonds come together, then place the remaining daisies 36 stitches away from the center daisy on each side, also on a point where two diamonds come together, until you get to the sides of the sweater.

Flip the garment over, and place daisies on the back in the same manner. The daisies are deliberately intended not to be symmetrical. Place the next row of daisies 15 rounds above the previous row of daisies, with each daisy centered between 2 daisies of the previous round. Continue in this manner, staggering the placement of each row of daisies, until you reach the shoulders.

Using a single strand of CA, embroider a French knot (see page 197) in the center of each first-row daisy.

Using CE, embroider French knots in the center of each second-row daisy.

Continue in this manner, alternating the color used for the French knots in each row of daisies.

For the sleeves, work two lazy daisies on the first Round 6 of Diamonds pattern, placing each daisy on either side of the center 36 stitches. Continue to embroider rows of sleeve daisies as for body.

Work French knots in the center of each sleeve daisy, beginning by using CC for the first-row daisies, and alternating CA and CC for each row thereafter.

Lazy daisy worked at point where diamonds come together, with French knot at center.

striped turtleneck in the round

reverse Stockinette Ridges of many contrasting shades are interspersed on a henna-colored pattern. The turtleneck, decorated with French knots, is added after the body is complete. The color choices make it perfect for an autumn walk in the woods — or a nap on your favorite couch.

Plan of action: Knitting in the round from the neck down makes it easy to match the stripes of the body and sleeves throughout the sweater. In the yoke, four increase rounds make the piece large enough to fit your upper body from neck to armholes. Then the work is divided into three sections: a body worked in the round and two sleeves each worked separately.

YARN

Nashua Handknits Julia, 50% wool/ 25% mohair/25% alpaca, 93 yd (85 m)/ 1¾ oz (50 g). Yarn band gauge: 5 stitches and 6 rows = 1" (2.5 cm) in Stockinette Stitch on US 7 (4.5 mm) needles.

CA = 2230 Rock Henna, 6 skeins for Extra-small, 7 skeins for Small, 8 skeins for Medium, 9 skeins for Large, 10 skeins for Extra-large

CB = 2163 Golden Honey, 2 skeins for Extra-small, Small, Medium, and Large; 3 skeins for Extra-large

CC = 3961 Ladies Mantle, 2 skeins for Extra-small; 3 skeins for Small, Medium, Large, and Extra-large

CD = 8141 Pretty Pink, 2 skeins for Extra-small, Small, Medium, and Large; 3 skeins for Extra-large

CE = 4936 Blue Thyme, 2 skeins for Extra-small, Small, Medium, and Large; 3 skeins for Extra-large

CF = 4330 Mushroom, 2 skeins for Extra-small, Small, Medium, and Large; 3 skeins for Extra-large

stitches

STRIPE PATTERN
Round 1 With CB, knit.
Round 2 With CB, purl.
Rounds 3 and 4 Repeat Rounds 1 and 2.
Rounds 5–8 With CA, knit.
Rounds 9–12 With CC, repeat Rounds 1–4.
Rounds 13–16 With CA, knit.
Rounds 17–20 With CD, repeat Rounds 1–4.
Rounds 21–24 With CA, knit.
Rounds 25–28 With CE, repeat Rounds 1–4.
Rounds 29–32 With CA, knit.
Rounds 33–36 With CF, repeat Rounds 1–4.
Rounds 37–40 With CA, knit.
Repeat Rounds 1–40 for pattern.

GARTER STITCH
Round 1 Knit.
Round 2 Purl.
Repeat these 2 rounds for pattern.

K3, P3 RIB
Work all rounds as *K3, P3; repeat from * to end of round.

SIZES AND FINISHED CHEST MEASUREMENTS

Extra-small 38" (96.5 cm), Small 42" (106.5 cm), Medium 46" (117 cm), Large 50" (127 cm), Extra-large 54" (137 cm). Model shown is size small.

GAUGE

17 stitches and 28 rounds = 4" (10 cm) in stripe pattern. (See Swatching in the Round, page 192.)

NEEDLES

US 8 (5 mm) circular needles 16" (40 cm) and 24" or 29" (60 or 75 cm) long *or size you need to obtain the correct gauge*

Set of four or five US 8 (5 mm) double-pointed needles *or size you need to obtain the correct gauge*

NOTIONS

Tapestry needle

Stitch marker

Stitch holders

Removable marker or safety pin

ABBREVIATIONS

K2tog = knit 2 stitches together

M1 = make one stitch (see page 200)

Ssk = Slip, slip, knit 2 together

To determine your gauge accurately, make sure you work your swatch in the round (see page 192). Wash the swatch and lay it flat to dry, pulling it gently lengthwise to counteract the garter ridges' tendencies to contract when they're first knit. As the sweater is worn, the garter ridges will relax and grow a bit vertically, so you want your swatch to account for this. Measure your gauge once the swatch is dry.

KNITTING THE YOKE	EXTRA-SMALL	SMALL	MEDIUM	LARGE	EXTRA-LARGE
Note When increasing for yoke, change to longer circular needle when there are too many stitches to fit comfortably around the shorter needle.					
Set Up With CA and shorter circular needle, cast on	68 sts	72 sts	76 sts	80 sts	84 sts
Place marker and join for working in the round, being careful not to twist stitches.					
Next 4 Rounds With CA, knit.					
Next Rounds Changing colors as indicated for pattern, work in Stripe Pattern until piece measures 1" (2.5 cm) from cast-on edge for all sizes, and end ready to work a knit round as the next round.					
First Increase Round Continuing in established Stripe Pattern and using the M1 increase method (see page 200), increase for your size as follows:					

Extra-small: *K2, M1, K3, M1; repeat from * to last 8 stitches, [K2, M1] 4 times.

Small: *K2, M1; repeat from * to end.

Medium: *K2, M1; repeat from * to last 4 stitches, K4.

Large: *K1, M1, [K2, M1] 3 times; repeat from * to last 3 stitches, K3.

KNITTING THE YOKE (CONT'D)	EXTRA-SMALL	SMALL	MEDIUM	LARGE	EXTRA-LARGE
Extra-large: *K1, M1, [K2, M1] 2 times; repeat from * to last 4 stitches, [K1, M1] 4 times.					
You now have	96 sts	108 sts	112 sts	124 sts	136 sts
Work even in established Stripe Pattern until piece measures from cast-on edge	3" (7.5 cm)	3¼" (8.5 cm)	3¼" (8.5 cm)	3½" (9 cm)	3½" (9 cm)
End ready to work a knit round as the next round.					

Second Increase Round Continuing in established Stripe Pattern, increase for your size as follows:

Extra-small, Small, and Medium: *K2, M1; repeat from * to end.

Large: *K2, M1; repeat from * to last 4 stitches, K4.

Extra-large: *K2, M1; repeat from * to end.

	EXTRA-SMALL	SMALL	MEDIUM	LARGE	EXTRA-LARGE
You now have	144 sts	162 sts	168 sts	184 sts	204 sts
Work even in established Stripe Pattern until piece measures from cast-on edge	5" (12.5 cm)	5½" (14 cm)	5½" (14 cm)	6" (15 cm)	6" (15 cm)
End ready to work a knit round as the next round.					

Third Increase Round Continuing in established Stripe Pattern, increase for your size as follows:

Extra-small: *K3, M1; repeat from * to last 6 stitches, K6.

Small and Medium: *K3, M1; repeat from * to end.

Large: *K3, M1; repeat from * to last 4 stitches, [K2, M1] 2 times.

Extra-large: *K3, M1; repeat from * to end.

	EXTRA-SMALL	SMALL	MEDIUM	LARGE	EXTRA-LARGE
You now have	190 sts	216 sts	224 sts	246 sts	272 sts
Work even in established Stripe Pattern until piece measures from cast-on edge	7¼" (18.5 cm)	7¾" (19.5 cm)	8" (20.5 cm)	8½" (21.5 cm)	8¾" (22 cm)
End ready to work a knit round as the next round.					

KNITTING THE YOKE (CONT'D)	EXTRA-SMALL	SMALL	MEDIUM	LARGE	EXTRA-LARGE

Fourth Increase Round Continuing in established Stripe Pattern, increase for your size as follows:

> *Extra-small:* *K3, M1, [K4, M1] 3 times; repeat from * to last 10 stitches, [K5, M1] 2 times.

> *Small and Medium:* *K4, M1; repeat from * to end.

> *Large:* *K4, M1; repeat from * to last 6 stitches, [K3, M1] 2 times.

> *Extra-large:* *K4, M1; repeat from * to end.

	EXTRA-SMALL	SMALL	MEDIUM	LARGE	EXTRA-LARGE
You now have	240 sts	270 sts	280 sts	308 sts	340 sts

Work even in established Stripe Pattern until piece measures from cast-on edge

	EXTRA-SMALL	SMALL	MEDIUM	LARGE	EXTRA-LARGE
	8½" (21.5 cm)	9¼" (23.5 cm)	9½" (24 cm)	10" (25.5 cm)	10½" (26.5 cm)

End having just finished a 4-round Garter Stitch Stripe.

Fifth Increase Round Using CA, work for your size as follows:

> *Extra-small:* *K120, M1; repeat from * once more.

> *Small:* *K135, M1; repeat from * once more.

> *Medium:* *K70, M1; repeat from * to end.

> *Large:* *K154, M1; repeat from * once more.

> *Extra-large:* Knit 1 round without increasing.

	EXTRA-SMALL	SMALL	MEDIUM	LARGE	EXTRA-LARGE
You now have	242 sts	272 sts	284 sts	310 sts	340 sts

Dividing Round Using CA and the Backward Loop Cast On (see page 200), divide stitches for body and sleeves as follows:

	EXTRA-SMALL	SMALL	MEDIUM	LARGE	EXTRA-LARGE
For back, knit	72 sts	81 sts	85 sts	94 sts	102 sts
Place on holder for sleeve	49 sts	55 sts	57 sts	61 sts	68 sts
Cast on for underarm	9 sts	9 sts	13 sts	13 sts	13 sts
For front knit	72 sts	81 sts	85 sts	94 sts	102 sts
Place on holder for second sleeve	49 sts	55 sts	57 sts	61 sts	68 sts
Cast on for second underarm	9 sts	9 sts	13 sts	13 sts	13 sts

back shaping

Some "knit-in-the-round" sweater patterns include directions for working short rows to build up the back neck, but I've always found this confusing and unnecessary. Here's my suggestion: tie a strand of wool or sew a label inside the sweater to indicate which side is the back. After you've worn the sweater a few times with the same side consistently in back, the wool will naturally conform to your body to create a comfortably fitting neck. If you're really committed to speeding up the process, spritz the back of the sweater and wear it while it's still damp; your own body heat will mold the wet wool beautifully.

KNITTING THE YOKE (CONT'D)	EXTRA-SMALL	SMALL	MEDIUM	LARGE	EXTRA-LARGE
Place marker to indicate new beginning of round. *You now have on longer circular needle for lower body*	162 sts	180 sts	196 sts	214 sts	230 sts
KNITTING THE LOWER BODY					
Knit 2 more rounds with CA to finish a 4-round Stockinette Stripe.					
Resume working in established Stripe Pattern until piece measures from cast-on edge	22" (56 cm)	23" (58.5 cm)	24" (61 cm)	24½" (62 cm)	25" (63.5 cm)
End having just finished a 4-round Garter Stitch Stripe.					
Change to CA, and work entirely in Garter Stitch for 8 rounds.					
Piece measures from cast-on edge about	23" (58.5 cm)	24" (61 cm)	25" (63.5 cm)	25½" (65 cm)	26" (66 cm)
Bind off all stitches.					
KNITTING THE SLEEVES					
Note When decreasing for sleeves, change to double-pointed needles if necessary when there are too few stitches to fit comfortably around the circular needle.					

KNITTING THE SLEEVES (CONT'D)	EXTRA-SMALL	SMALL	MEDIUM	LARGE	EXTRA-LARGE
Set Up Return stitches for one sleeve to shorter circular needle. Join CA to beginning of stitches with right side facing.					
You now have	49 sts	55 sts	57 sts	61 sts	68 sts
Next Round					
Knit to the end of the sleeve stitches.					
Use the Backward Loop Cast On to cast on	4 sts	4 sts	6 sts	6 sts	6 sts
Cast on 1 more stitch and place a removable marker or safety pin directly in this stitch.					
Use the Loop Cast on to cast on	4 sts	4 sts	6 sts	6 sts	6 sts
You now have	58 sts	64 sts	70 sts	74 sts	81 sts
The marked stitch is the new first stitch of the round.					
Knit 1 more round with CA to finish a 4-round Stockinette Stripe.					
Resume working in established Stripe Pattern until piece measures 1" (2.5 cm) from dividing round.					
Note Work all sleeve decrease rounds on a knit round; reposition the removable marker every so often as you work, so the first stitch is always clearly marked.					
***Decrease Round** K1 (marked stitch), K2tog, knit to last 2 stitches of round, ssk: 2 stitches decreased.					
Work even in established Stripe Pattern until piece measures from decrease round	1¼" (3.2 cm)	1" (2.5 cm)	1" (2.5 cm)	1" (2.5 cm)	1" (2.5 cm)
End ready to work a knit round as the next round.					
Repeat from * at beginning of decrease round	10 more times	12 more times	14 more times	15 more times	17 more times
You now have	36 sts	38 sts	40 sts	42 sts	45 sts

KNITTING THE SLEEVES (CONT'D)	EXTRA-SMALL	SMALL	MEDIUM	LARGE	EXTRA-LARGE
Repeat the decrease round once more on the next knit round.					
You now have	34 sts	36 sts	38 sts	40 sts	43 sts
Continue even in established Stripe Pattern until sleeve measures from dividing round about	16¼" (41.5 cm)	17½" (44.5 cm)	18¾" (47.5 cm)	19½" (49.5 cm)	19¾" (50 cm)
End having just finished a 4-round Garter Stitch Stripe.					
Change to CA, and work entirely in Garter Stitch for 8 rounds.					
Sleeve measures from dividing round about	17¼" (44 cm)	18½" (47 cm)	19¾" (50 cm)	20½" (52 cm)	20¾" (52.5 cm)
Bind off all stitches.					
Return held stitches for second sleeve to shorter circular needle and work as for first sleeve.					
KNITTING THE TURTLE-NECK					
Set Up With color of your choice (CC shown here) and shorter circular needle, pick up and knit around neck opening	68 sts	72 sts	76 sts	80 sts	84 sts
Place marker and join for working in the round.					
Next Round Knit 1 round, decreasing evenly	2 sts	0 sts	4 sts	2 sts	0 sts
You now have	66 sts	72 sts	72 sts	78 sts	84 sts
Next Rounds Work in K3, P3 Rib until turtleneck measures 6" (15 cm) from pickup round, or desired length.					
Bind off all stitches loosely in rib pattern.					

FINISHING

Sew underarm seams closed. Weave in ends.

EMBROIDERY

Fold turtleneck down to identify the right, or public, side of the bind-off edge when turtleneck is worn.

Using a single strand of CA, embroider a French knot (see page 197) in the center of K3 rib column on right side of turtleneck about ½" (1.3 cm) away from bind-off edge as shown. Do not cut CA after each knot. Instead, skim the yarn loosely along the wrong side of the turtleneck to the next French knot position, catching just a single ply of the rib fabric, and matching the stretch of the turtleneck.

French knots worked at center of stockinette ridges on ribbed turtleneck.

color alternatives

Turtleneck. Once the sweater is finished, choose your favorite color for the turtleneck (I picked my favorite, Lady's Mantle). Pick up and knit stitches from around the cast-on edge of the neck opening (the stitch count should be divisible by 6), and work the turtleneck to your own taste, long or short.

Stripes. The textured stripe pattern for this pullover is easy to memorize: 4 rounds of Stockinette in the main color, then 4 rounds of Garter Stitch in one of the contrast colors. You could easily make this sweater using only one contrast color for a two–color effect, or use a single color throughout (pick a lighter color for this option, if you want the garter stitch stripes to show up nicely).

embroidered
fair isle
cardigan

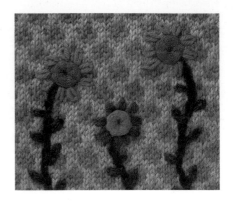

mismatched geometric patterns combined with floral embroidery make for a fabulous zippered cardigan. Truly a challenging project, but worth any knitter's time and talents!

Plan of action: The body of the sweater is worked in the round to the shoulders with steeked sections for the armholes and front neck. During finishing, the steeks are secured with machine stitching then cut open. For easier identification, work steek stitches in stockinette (knit every round), even on rounds that include Reverse Stockinette Ridges. The sleeves are worked separately in the round and sewn into cut armhole openings. Finally the mitered edging is worked in the round on stitches picked up from around the entire edge of the body.

YARN

Nashua Handknits Julia, 50% wool/25% mohair/25% alpaca, 93 yd (85 m)/1¾ oz (50 g). Yarn band gauge: 5 stitches and 6 rows = 1" (2.5 cm) in Stockinette Stitch on US 7 (4.5 mm) needles.

CA = 2230 Rock Henna, 2 skeins for Extra-small, Small, and Medium; 3 skeins for Large and Extra-large

CB = 1220 Tarnished Brass, 2 skeins for Extra-small, Small, and Medium; 3 skeins for Large and Extra-Large

CC = 9235 Anemone, 2 skeins for Extra-small, Small, and Medium; 3 skeins for Large and Extra-Large

CD = 3961 Ladies Mantle, 3 skeins for Extra-small, Small, and Medium; 4 skeins for Large and Extra-large

CE = 4936 Blue Thyme, 3 skeins for Extra-small, Small, and Medium; 4 skeins for Large; 5 skeins for Extra-large

CF = 8118 Espresso, 4 skeins for Extra-small, Small, and Medium; 5 skeins for Large; 6 skeins for Extra-large

CG = 6396 Deep Blue Sea, 1 skein for Extra-small, Small, and Medium; 2 skeins for Large and Extra-large

CH = 1784 Gourd, 4 skeins for Extra-small; 5 skeins for Small and Medium; 6 skeins for Large; 7 skeins for Extra-large

ABBREVIATIONS

Dec = decrease 1 stitch
Inc = increase 1 stitch
K2tog = knit 2 stitches together
M1 = make 1 stitch (see page 200)
Ssk = slip, slip, knit these 2 stitches together

stitches

> **REVERSE STOCKINETTE RIDGE**
> **Round 1** Knit.
> **Rounds 2 and 3** Purl.
>
> **STOCKINETTE STITCH IN THE ROUND**
> Knit all stitches every round.

SIZES AND FINISHED CHEST MEASUREMENTS

Extra-small 34" (86.5 cm), Small 38" (96.5 cm), Medium 42" (106.5 cm), Large 46" (117 cm), Extra-large 50" (127 cm). Model shown is size medium.

GAUGE

20 stitches and 22 rounds = 4" (10 cm) in Stockinette Stitch colorwork pattern from charts worked in the round using largest needles.

NEEDLES

US 7 (4.5 mm) circular needle 24" or 29" (60 or 75 cm) long *or size you need to obtain the correct gauge*

US 6 (4 mm) circular needle 24" or 29" (60 or 75 cm) long

Set of four or five US 7 (4.5 mm) double-pointed needles *or size you need to obtain the correct gauge*

Set of four or five US 6 (4 mm) double-pointed needles

Three US 5 (3.75 mm) circular needles 29" (60 or 75 cm) long for mitered edging

NOTIONS

Tapestry needle

Stitch markers

24" (61 cm) or longer separating zipper to match outermost edging color (CF for sweater shown)

Sewing machine for sewing steeks (optional)

Sewing needle and matching thread for sewing steeks and attaching zipper

KNITTING THE BODY	EXTRA-SMALL	SMALL	MEDIUM	LARGE	EXTRA-LARGE
Set Up With CA and medium-size circular needle, cast on	174 sts	194 sts	214 sts	234 sts	254 sts
Place marker and join for working in the round, being careful not to twist stitches.					
Round 1 Establish position of steeks as follows:					
K3 stitches for half of center front steek.					
Place marker					
Knit for right front	42 sts	47 sts	52 sts	57 sts	62 sts
Place marker for right side.					
Knit for back	84 sts	94 sts	104 sts	114 sts	124 sts
Place marker for left side.					
Knit for left front	42 sts	47 sts	52 sts	57 sts	62 sts
Place marker.					
K3 stitches for half of center front steek.					
Note The first and last 3 stitches of every round are knit for the remainder of the sweater body in order to identify the steek stitches.					
Rounds 2–5 With CA, knit.					
Rounds 6–9 Change to largest circular needle. Using CA and CB as shown, work Rounds 1–4 of Flower Centers for Body Chart. The first and last 3 stitches of the chart are the steek stitches and are worked in alternating colors as shown on chart.					
Rounds 10–14 Change to medium-size circular needle. With CA, knit.					
Rounds 15–17 Change to CC and work 1 Reverse Stockinette Ridge, working 3 steek stitches at each end of round in stockinette, and decreasing evenly in Round 17	0 sts	2 sts	4 sts	0 sts	2 sts
You now have	174 sts	192 sts	210 sts	234 sts	252 sts
Piece measures about 2½" (6.5 cm) from cast-on edge.					

	EXTRA-SMALL	SMALL	MEDIUM	LARGE	EXTRA-LARGE
Rounds 18–61 Change to largest circular needle. Using CD and CE as shown, repeat Rounds 1–8 of Dots Chart five times, then work Rounds 1–4 of chart once more: 44 total rounds completed from Dots Chart.					
Piece measures about 10½" (26.5 cm) from cast-on edge.					
Rounds 62–64 Change to medium–size circular needle. With CF, work 1 Reverse Stockinette Ridge, working 3 steek stitches at each end of round in stockinette, and increasing evenly in Round 62	0 sts	2 sts	4 sts	0 sts	2 sts
You now have	174 sts	194 sts	214 sts	234 sts	254 sts
Rounds 65–67 Change to CB and work 1 Reverse Stockinette Ridge, working 3 steek stitches at each end of round in stockinette, and evenly in Round 67	inc 2 sts	dec 1 st	dec 0 sts	dec 3 sts	dec 2 sts
You now have	176 sts	193 sts	214 sts	231 sts	252 sts
Rounds 68–70 With CC, knit.					
Rounds 71–80 Change to largest circular needle. Using CC and CG as shown, work Rounds 1–10 of Linked Circles Chart, working the single marked stitch at each side of chart between the main pattern repeat and the steek stitches as indicated for your size	0 times	0 times	2 times	2 times	4 times
Rounds 81–83 Change to medium-size circular needle. With CC, knit.					
Rounds 84–86 Change to CB and work 1 Reverse Stockinette Ridge, working 3 steek stitches at each end of round in stockinette, and evenly in Round 84	dec 2 sts	inc 1 st	inc 0 sts	inc 3 sts	inc 2 sts
You now have	174 sts	194 sts	214 sts	234 sts	254 sts
Piece measures about 14½" (37 cm) from cast-on edge.					

KNITTING THE BODY
(CONT'D)

Round 87 Change to largest circular needle. With CF and CH, establish pattern from Round 1 of Zigzag Knitting Chart for your size as follows:

Extra-small: Work 3 steek stitches once, work stitch 21 to stitch 26 of pattern repeat once, work entire 26–stitch pattern repeat 6 times, work stitch 1 to stitch 6 of pattern repeat once, work 3 steek stitches once.

Small: Work 3 steek stitches once, work stitch 24 to stitch 26 of pattern repeat once, work entire 26–stitch pattern repeat 7 times, work stitch 1 to stitch 3 of pattern repeat once, work 3 steek stitches once.

Medium: Work 3 steek stitches once, work entire 26–stitch pattern repeat 8 times, work 3 steek stitches once.

Large: Work 3 steek stitches once, work stitch 17 to stitch 26 of pattern repeat once, work entire 26–stitch pattern repeat 8 times, work stitch 1 to stitch 10 of pattern repeat once, work 3 steek stitches once.

Extra-large: Work 3 steek stitches once, work stitch 20 to stitch 26 of pattern repeat once, work entire 26–stitch pattern repeat 8 times, work stitch 1 to stitch 7 of pattern repeat once, work 3 steek stitches once.

Rounds 88 and 89 Work chart Rounds 2 and 3 in pattern as established.

Piece measures about 15" (38) from cast-on edge.

Round 90 Work Round 4 of chart in pattern as established, and cast on for armhole steeks as follows:

Work in pattern from chart to right side seam marker and slip marker.

Whenever a color is not used for five or more stitches in any charted sections, twist the unused color together with the working color to catch it against the back of the fabric (see page 192). See pages 191 and 195 for instructions on working from a chart.

KNITTING THE BODY (CONT'D)	EXTRA-SMALL	SMALL	MEDIUM	LARGE	EXTRA-LARGE
Using the Backward Loop method (see page 200), cast on 6 stitches as follows: *1 stitch CF, 1 stitch CH; repeat from * two more times for right armhole steek.					
Place new marker.					
Work in pattern from chart to left side seam marker and slip marker.					
Using the Backward Loop method, cast on 6 stitches as follows: *1 stitch CF, 1 stitch CH; repeat from * two more times for left armhole steek.					
Place new marker.					
Work in pattern to end of round.					
You now have	186 sts	206 sts	226 sts	246 sts	266 sts
Each front has	42 sts	47 sts	52 sts	57 sts	62 sts
Back has	84 sts	94 sts	104 sts	114 sts	124 sts
Each armhole steek has	6 sts	6 sts	6 sts	6 sts	6 sts
Center front steek has at each end of round	3 sts	3 sts	3 sts	3 sts	3 sts
Next Rounds Working marked groups of steek stitches in alternating colors as for center front steek, continue in established pattern from Zigzag Knitting Chart on fronts and back until piece measures from cast-on edge	20½" (52 cm)	21" (53.5 cm)	21½" (54.5 cm)	22" (56 cm)	22½" (57 cm)

Shape Front Neck

	EXTRA-SMALL	SMALL	MEDIUM	LARGE	EXTRA-LARGE
Next Round Continue in established patterns from chart and for steeks, and work until there remain at end of round	14 sts	15 sts	15 sts	16 sts	17 sts
Next Round Using CH, bind off for center front neck as follows, removing end-of-round marker when you come to it:					
Bind off from previous round last	14 sts	15 sts	15 sts	16 sts	17 sts
Then bind off from this round the first	14 sts	15 sts	15 sts	16 sts	17 sts

Shape Front Neck (CONT'D)	EXTRA-SMALL	SMALL	MEDIUM	LARGE	EXTRA-LARGE
Work in established patterns to end of round.					
You now have for each front	31 sts	35 sts	40 sts	44 sts	48 sts

Next Round Continue in established patterns, and cast on for new center front steek as follows:

Using the Backward Loop method, cast on 3 stitches as follows: 1 stitch CF, 1 stitch CH, 1 stitch CF.

Place marker for center front and new beginning of round.

Using the Backward Loop method, cast on 3 stitches as follows: 1 stitch CH, 1 stitch CF, 1 stitch CH.

Work in established patterns to end, then work first 3 steek stitches once more to end at new marker for beginning of round.

	EXTRA-SMALL	SMALL	MEDIUM	LARGE	EXTRA-LARGE
You now have	164 sts	182 sts	202 sts	220 sts	238 sts
Each front has	31 sts	35 sts	40 sts	44 sts	48 sts
Back has	84 sts	94 sts	104 sts	114 sts	124 sts
Each armhole steek has	6 sts	6 sts	6 sts	6 sts	6 sts
Center front steek has at each end of round	3 sts	3 sts	3 sts	3 sts	3 sts

Work new center front steek stitches in alternating colors as for other steeks.

Decrease Round Continuing in established patterns, work 3 steek stitches, ssk, work in pattern to last 5 stitches of round, K2tog, work 3 steek stitches: 2 stitches decreased, 1 on either side of center front steek.

Next Round Work 1 round even in established patterns.

Next 6 Rounds Repeat the last 2 rounds 3 more times.

	EXTRA-SMALL	SMALL	MEDIUM	LARGE	EXTRA-LARGE
You now have	156 sts	174 sts	194 sts	212 sts	230 sts
Each front has	27 sts	31 sts	36 sts	40 sts	44 sts
Back has	84 sts	94 sts	104 sts	114 sts	124 sts
Each armhole steek has	6 sts	6 sts	6 sts	6 sts	6 sts

Shape Front Neck (CONT'D)

	EXTRA-SMALL	SMALL	MEDIUM	LARGE	EXTRA-LARGE
Center front steek has at each end of round	3 sts	3 sts	3 sts	3 sts	3 sts
Work even in established patterns until piece measures from cast-on edge	22½" (57 cm)	23" (58.5 cm)	23½" (59.5 cm)	24" (61 cm)	24½" (62 cm)

Next 3 Rounds Change to medium-size circular needle. With CE, work 1 Reverse Stockinette Ridge, working all steek stitches in stockinette.

	EXTRA-SMALL	SMALL	MEDIUM	LARGE	EXTRA-LARGE
Armholes measure from beginning of armhole steeks about	8" (20.5 cm)	8½" (21.5 cm)	9" (23 cm)	9½" (24 cm)	10" (25.5 cm)

Bind off all stitches.

KNITTING THE SLEEVES

Note When increasing for the sleeves, change to shorter circular needle in the indicated size when there are too many stitches to fit comfortably around the double-pointed needles.

	EXTRA-SMALL	SMALL	MEDIUM	LARGE	EXTRA-LARGE
Set Up and Round 1 With CG and smaller double-pointed needles, cast on	38 sts	40 sts	42 sts	44 sts	46 sts

The cast on counts as Round 1 of Stripe pattern. Divide stitches as evenly as possible on three needles, place marker and join for working in the round, being careful not to twist stitches.

Rounds 2 and 3 With CG, purl.

Rounds 4–6 With CB, work 1 Reverse Stockinette Ridge.

Rounds 7–9 With CA, work 1 Reverse Stockinette Ridge.

	EXTRA-SMALL	SMALL	MEDIUM	LARGE	EXTRA-LARGE
Rounds 10–12 With CF, work 1 Reverse Stockinette Ridge, and evenly in Round 12 increase	7 sts	7 sts	8 sts	6 sts	4 sts
You now have	45 sts	47 sts	50 sts	50 sts	50 sts

Rounds 13–17 With CD, knit.

KNITTING THE SLEEVES (CONT'D)	EXTRA-SMALL	SMALL	MEDIUM	LARGE	EXTRA-LARGE

Round 18 Change to larger double-pointed needles. With CD and CC, establish pattern from Round 1 of Flower Centers for Sleeve Chart for your size as follows:

Extra-small: Work 1 edge stitch, work stitch 9 to stitch 10 of pattern repeat once, work entire 10-stitch pattern repeat 4 times, work stitch 1 of pattern repeat once more, work 1 edge stitch.

Small: Work 1 edge stitch, work stitch 8 to stitch 10 of pattern repeat once, work entire 10-stitch pattern repeat 4 times, work stitch 1 to stitch 2 of pattern repeat once more, work 1 edge stitch.

Medium, Large, and Extra-large: Work 1 edge stitch, work entire 10-stitch pattern repeat 5 times, work 1 edge stitch.

Rounds 19–21 With CD and CC, work Rounds 2–4 of chart.

Rounds 22–26 Change to smaller double-pointed needles. With CD, knit.

Rounds 27–29 With CB, work 1 Reverse Stockinette Ridge.

| **Rounds 30–32** With CF, work 1 Reverse Stockinette Ridge, and evenly in Round 32 increase | 15 sts | 13 sts | 15 sts | 15 sts | 15 sts |
| *You now have* | 60 sts | 60 sts | 65 sts | 65 sts | 65 sts |

Piece measures about 4¼" (11 cm) from cast-on edge.

Round 32 Change to larger double-pointed needles. With CF and CH, establish pattern from Round 1 of Circles Chart for your size as follows:

Extra-small and Small: Work 1 edge stitch, work stitch 7 to stitch 10 of pattern repeat once, work entire 10-stitch pattern repeat 5 times, work stitch 1 to stitch 4 of pattern repeat once, work 1 edge stitch.

KNITTING THE SLEEVES (CONT'D)	EXTRA-SMALL	SMALL	MEDIUM	LARGE	EXTRA-LARGE
Medium, Large, and Extra-large: Work 1 edge stitch, work stitch 9 to stitch 10 of pattern repeat once, work entire 10-stitch pattern repeat 6 times, work stitch 1 of pattern repeat once more, work 1 edge stitch.					
Increase Round Continuing in established pattern, increase 1 stitch at each end of round as follows: Work 1 edge stitch, M1, work in pattern to last stitch, M1, work 1 edge: 2 stitches increased.					
Next Rounds Continuing in pattern, and working new stitches into Circles pattern from chart, work increase round every 4th round	9 times	12 times	12 times	14 times	17 times
You now have	80 sts	86 sts	91 sts	95 sts	101 sts
Next Rounds Continue in pattern until piece measures from cast-on edge	14" (35.5 cm)	15" (38 cm)	16" (40.5 cm)	17" (43 cm)	18" (45.5 cm)
Bind off all stitches.					

SECURING AND CUTTING THE STEEKS

Secure the steeks for cutting as shown on page 203:

Using sewing machine set to zigzag stitch, stitch down the middle of the stitches on each side of the center of the armhole steeks.

Using sewing machine set to straight stitch, sew in the ditch between the main pattern and steek stitches on each side of armhole steeks.

Carefully cut the armholes open along the center of the steeks from bound-off edge to beginning of steeks.

Secure and cut center front and front neck steeks in the same manner.

MITERED EDGING	EXTRA-SMALL	SMALL	MEDIUM	LARGE	EXTRA-LARGE

Using CE, sew shoulder seams.

Note Edging is worked in the round on stitches from around the entire edge of the body. Stitches are divided onto 2 smallest-size circular needles and worked using the third smallest-size needle. You may find it helpful to use a different colored marker to indicate the beginning of the round.

Set Up and Round 1 Using CD and one or more smallest circular needle, beginning at cast-on edge of left front, pick up and knit stitches from body as follows:

Pick up and knit 1 stitch in corner of lower left front, place marker.

	EXTRA-SMALL	SMALL	MEDIUM	LARGE	EXTRA-LARGE
Pick up and knit around entire cast-on edge of body (1 stitch for every cast-on stitch, not including front steeks)	168 sts	188 sts	208 sts	228 sts	248 sts

Place marker, pick up and knit 1 stitch in corner of lower right front, place marker.

	EXTRA-SMALL	SMALL	MEDIUM	LARGE	EXTRA-LARGE
Pick up and knit along right front opening to beginning of neck shaping	90 sts	92 sts	94 sts	96 sts	98 sts

Place marker, pick up and knit 1 stitch in corner of right front neck, place marker.

	EXTRA-SMALL	SMALL	MEDIUM	LARGE	EXTRA-LARGE
Pick up and knit around neck opening	68 sts	73 sts	73 sts	76 sts	81 sts

Place marker, pick up and knit 1 stitch in corner of left front neck, place marker.

	EXTRA-SMALL	SMALL	MEDIUM	LARGE	EXTRA-LARGE
Pick up and knit along left front opening	90 sts	92 sts	94 sts	96 sts	98 sts

Place marker and join for working in the round

	EXTRA-SMALL	SMALL	MEDIUM	LARGE	EXTRA-LARGE
You now have	420 sts	449 sts	473 sts	500 sts	529 sts

MITERED EDGING (CONT'D)	EXTRA-SMALL	SMALL	MEDIUM	LARGE	EXTRA-LARGE
Round 2 With CD, K1 (corner stitch), M1, *purl to next corner stitch, M1, K1 (corner stitch), M1; repeat from * 2 more times, purl to last corner stitch, M1, K1:	8 sts increased	8 sts increased	8 sts increased	8 sts increased	8 sts increased
You now have	428 sts	457 sts	481 sts	508 sts	537 sts
Round 3 With CD, *K1 (corner stitch), purl to next corner stitch; repeat from * 3 more times.					
Round 4 Change to CC. K1 (corner stitch), M1, *knit to next corner stitch, M1, K1 (corner stitch), M1; repeat from * 2 more times, knit to last corner stitch, M1, K1:	8 sts increased	8 sts increased	8 sts increased	8 sts increased	8 sts increased
You now have	436 sts	465 sts	489 sts	516 sts	545 sts
Round 5 With CC, repeat Round 3.					
Round 6 With CC, repeat Round 2:	8 sts increased	8 sts increased	8 sts increased	8 sts increased	8 sts increased
You now have	444 sts	473 sts	497 sts	524 sts	553 sts
Round 7 Change to CH. Knit.					
Round 8 With CH, repeat Round 2:	8 sts increased	8 sts increased	8 sts increased	8 sts increased	8 sts increased
You now have	452 sts	481 sts	505 sts	532 sts	561 sts
Round 9 With CH, repeat Round 3.					
Round 10 Change to CF. Repeat Round 4:	8 sts increased	8 sts increased	8 sts increased	8 sts increased	8 sts increased
You now have	460 sts	489 sts	513 sts	540 sts	569 sts
Round 11 With CF, repeat Round 3.					
Round 12 With CF, bind off all stitches as if to purl on this round.					

FINISHING

Sew sleeves into armholes. Weave in ends.

EMBROIDERY

Note The embroidery stitches are presented in order from the bottom of the sweater upwards to shoulders, and then for the sleeve cuffs.

For flower centers of body. Use a single strand of CE to work eight lazy daisies (see page 197) around each CB flower center, making slightly shorter petals between the flowers in order to fit, and longer petals at the top and bottom of each flower.

Lazy daisy petals around flower centers on body.

In Dots pattern. Use a single strand of CF to embroider wavy stems of varying lengths in chain stitch (see page 197) as shown. At the top of each stem, work flower heads of different sizes in spider web stitch (see page 198) using single strands of CC and CH, alternating colors for each flower. Around each flower head, embroider petals in lazy daisy stitch, using a single strand of CA around the CH flower heads, and CH around the CC flower heads. Using a single strand of CG, embroider alternating leaves in lazy daisy stitch on both sides of each flower stem.

Lazy daisy petals around spider web stitch center.

In Reverse Stockinette Ridges above Dots pattern. Embroider French knots (see page 197) using a single strand of CH, and spacing the knots so there are about 2½ knit stitches between each pair of knots.

In Linked Circles Pattern. Use a single strand of CD to work 10 evenly spaced French knots around the inside of each circle.

Between Reverse Stockinette Ridges above Linked Circles pattern. Embroider French knots using a single strand of CA, and spacing the knots about 2½ knit stitches apart as before.

French knots within linked circles motif.

In Zigzag pattern. Work duplicate stitch (see page 194) embroidery according to the Zigzag Embroidery Chart. Using a single strand of yarn, outline the zigzags with CE, then fill the centers of the small diamonds using a single strand of CB or CD as shown on chart.

On Cuffs. In the Flower Centers for Sleeves section use a single strand of CG to work eight lazy daisies around each CC flower center as for lower section of body on cuff.

In Circles pattern. Use a single strand of CE to embroider French knots along Round 1, placing the knots at the base of Stitch 1 and Stitch 6 of the pattern in the center of each 3-stitch dark block.

Lazy daisy petals around circles on cuff.

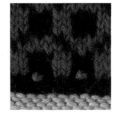

French knot at top of cuff.

ZIPPER

Using sewing needle and thread, insert zipper according to instructions on pages 205–206, adjusting zipper length for your size as given in directions.

POMPOM

Make a pompom (see page 199) about 2½" (6.5 cm) in diameter using CB, CC, CF, and CH. Cut 10" (25.5 cm) strands of CB, CC, and CF, and braid these strands together. Attach one end of the braid to the pompom. Slip the other end of the braid through the zipper pull, and secure end of braid with an overhand knot. Trim ends of braid.

center back **(FLOWERS PATTERN, RIGHT FRONT AND BACK)** center front

Repeat this pattern as a mirror image for left front and back.

EMBROIDERED FAIR ISLE CARDIGAN SCHEMATIC

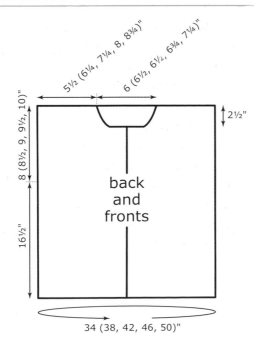

5½ (6¼, 7¼, 8, 8¾)"

6 (6½, 6½, 6¾, 7¼)"

8 (8½, 9, 9½, 10)"

2½"

16½"

back and fronts

34 (38, 42, 46, 50)"

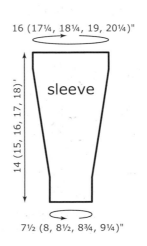

16 (17¼, 18¼, 19, 20¼)"

14 (15, 16, 17, 18)"

sleeve

7½ (8, 8½, 8¾, 9¼)"

EMBROIDERED FAIR ISLE CARDIGAN CHARTS

- ■ CA ROCK HENNA
- ■ CB TARNISHED BRASS
- ■ CC ANEMONE
- ■ CD LADIES MANTLE

- ■ CE BLUE THYME
- ■ CF ESPRESSO
- ■ CG DEEP BLUE SEA
- ■ CH GOURD

FLOWER CENTERS FOR BODY CHART

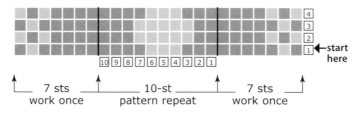

4
3
2
1 ←start here

10 9 8 7 6 5 4 3 2 1

7 sts work once   10-st pattern repeat   7 sts work once

DOTS CHART

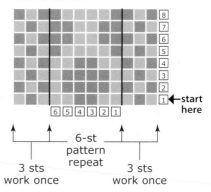

8
7
6
5
4
3
2
1 ←start here

6 5 4 3 2 1

6-st pattern repeat

3 sts work once   3 sts work once

LINKED CIRCLES CHART

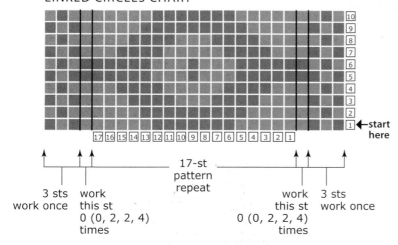

10
9
8
7
6
5
4
3
2
1 ←start here

17 16 15 14 13 12 11 10 9 8 7 6 5 4 3 2 1

17-st pattern repeat

3 sts work once   work this st 0 (0, 2, 2, 4) times   work this st 0 (0, 2, 2, 4) times   3 sts work once

ZIGZAG KNITTING CHART

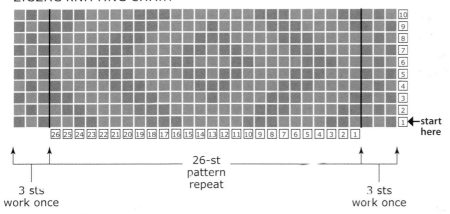

26 25 24 23 22 21 20 19 18 17 16 15 14 13 12 11 10 9 8 7 6 5 4 3 2 1

← start here

10 9 8 7 6 5 4 3 2 1

3 sts work once

26-st pattern repeat

3 sts work once

ZIGZAG EMBROIDERY CHART

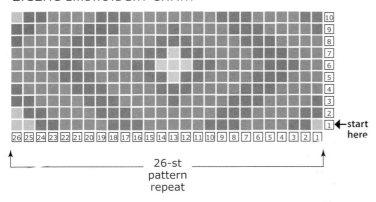

26 25 24 23 22 21 20 19 18 17 16 15 14 13 12 11 10 9 8 7 6 5 4 3 2 1

← start here

10 9 8 7 6 5 4 3 2 1

26-st pattern repeat

FLOWER CENTERS FOR SLEEVE CHART

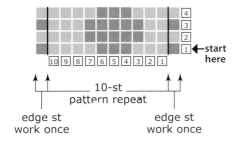

10 9 8 7 6 5 4 3 2 1

← start here

4 3 2 1

10-st pattern repeat

edge st work once

edge st work once

CIRCLES CHART

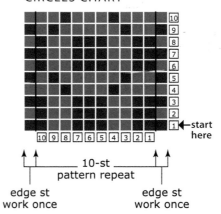

10 9 8 7 6 5 4 3 2 1

← start here

10 9 8 7 6 5 4 3 2 1

10-st pattern repeat

edge st work once

edge st work once

Back Down to Basics

My knitwear designs include many traditional knitting techniques developed years ago by knitters who knit before I was born and lived very far from where I live now. These techniques traveled from knitter to knitter, culture to culture, and are offered here for your use. As you knit your way through these patterns and practice these techniques, think about the knitters who came before you. They didn't have smooth store-bought needles to knit with, graph paper to make charts on, sewing machines to secure their fabric before cutting a steek, or books from

which to learn. Most knitters had to spin and dye their own yarn. They warmly dressed their families, and passed their knowledge onto their children and neighbors, helping them through their questions and mistakes.

As a knitwear designer, I have developed my own colorful style, with roots in historic and ethnic costumes and fabrics. I hope you'll practice these time-honored techniques and then tweek them to make your own signature style. Some may be new to you, some you may already know, but none is difficult. So, grab some yarn, some needles, and begin!

knitting with more than one color: Fair Isle

Knitting with two colors in the same row or round is traditionally called *Fair Isle knitting*. When I knit my first Fair Isle sweater 20-something years ago, I made the classic mistake every knitter does when first learning to knit with two colors: I pulled the non-working yarn too tightly across the back of the fabric when I was knitting with the other color. The pattern was an "in-the-round-yoke sweater," and by the time I was finished, I had a bunchy, tight yoke that I could barely fit my shoulders into. I wore the sweater anyway, but it was never very comfortable. From that experience, I learned to loosely carry the yarn not being worked at the back of the knitting. This ensures

It's tradition. Ethnic colors and patterns often influence and inspire my designs.

that your fabric will have some spring and give and be comfortable to wear.

You'll find that every time you pick up a Fair Isle project, your tension will be a little different, depending on the day, what happened, and how wound up you are. Try to pick up your knitting and let your cares slip away as you carry the colors across the back of the work. You'll end up with a better-fitting project.

Fair Isle patterns are usually presented as charted designs on graph paper, with each colored square standing for a stitch. You follow the chart square by square and line by line for guidance on what color to use for each stitch. You then repeat the chart a certain number of times for each row or round. As you proceed up the chart, a two- (or more) color pattern forms. Although this may sound completely complicated and overwhelming, it isn't! See A Chart to Practice With (page 192) to get you started.

Almost all of the projects in this book are worked in the round, so that you work with the right side of the fabric facing you and follow the chart from right to left, just as the stitches are arranged on your needle. (In projects that are worked in rows rather than rounds, you work the right-side rows from right to left on the chart and the wrong-side rows from left to right.)

When you are just beginning to learn to knit in the Fair Isle technique, you may find it helpful to mark each pattern repeat with stitch markers. For instance, if you have a 20-stitch repeat, place stitch markers every 20 stitches so that you know each time you have completed a full repeat. After a few rounds, as the pattern builds, you'll begin to know the pattern intimately and can probably remove the stitch markers.

Right or wrong? The lower photo shows the wrong side of the Fair Isle pattern above it. Note how the yarns are carried loosely, to avoid having the fabric bunch up.

A LITTLE QUIET THINKING

To be honest, I find stitch markers a nuisance, so I usually just sit myself down somewhere quiet for the first few rounds of every sweater until I get to know the pattern, and then I'm set. I find that after I've worked a complete pattern, I can anticipate the color changes and only have to refer occasionally to the chart as I work up the rest of the garment.

HANDLING "FLOATS"

Sometimes a color in a pattern is not used for many stitches, causing a "float" to develop across the back of the work. There's nothing worse than getting your fingers and rings stuck in a long float when you're trying to put on a sweater or pair of mittens. To avoid long floats, the traditional rule is to twist the yarn not being knit with every fifth stitch. This is as simple as it sounds: simply twist the working yarn around the non-working yarn to catch it into the fabric. (Do not "double-twist": one twist is enough.) Stretch the fabric on the right-hand needle as you do this to ensure that

A SWATCH IN THE ROUND: A CHART TO PRACTICE WITH

You will need two colors of worsted-weight yarn: Use CA (color A: blue) for the cast on and CB (color B: gold) for the second color. Using US 6 or 7 (4 or 4.5 mm) double-point needles, cast on 28 stitches and divide them evenly among 3 or 4 needles. (For advice on knitting in the round, refer to the section on double-point needles on page 201.) Now, follow the chart below, beginning with line 1 (Round 1) at the bottom right, and proceed as follows:

■ CA LUPINE
■ CB GOLDEN HONEY

1. With CA, knit 2 stitches.

2. Change to CB and knit 2 stitches.

3. Begin repeating the 4-stitch sequence you just knit. While stretching out the stitches you just knit, knit 2 with CA. As you carry CA across the back of the CB stitches, make sure to keep the strand of CA loose. This will ensure that the fabric doesn't bunch up and pull in.

4. Repeat this sequence around the entire swatch, always taking care to stretch out the stitches on the right-hand needle before knitting the next color. You have now completed line 1 of the chart.

5. For Round 2, follow line 2 of the chart, reading from the right. (Notice that on this chart, line 2 has the same color pattern as line 1.)

6. For Rounds 3 and 4, follow lines 3 and 4 of the chart. You have now completed 1 pattern repeat. Keep working to develop the checkerboard pattern by repeating rounds 1–4.

Avoiding floats. If your color change doesn't occur for more than 5 stitches, wrap the carried yarn around the working yarn to tuck it in and avoid a long "float" on the back of the work.

you're carrying the non-working yarn loosely across the back. The backside of the fabric will be neat and you won't have to worry about snagging a long float of yarn.

Some knitters twist their yarns every stitch, but I prefer not to because I think this makes the fabric too stiff. You may want to experiment and try it. The backside of the fabric will have an almost woven appearance. This is totally a matter of personal preference, so do what you like and what makes you most comfortable.

TWO-HANDED KNITTING

The most efficient way to approach two-color knitting is to learn to knit with both hands. I call this "wrapping and picking." Hold one color yarn in your right hand and wrap it around the needle American-style. Hold the other color in your left hand so that you can "pick" it, continental style. You'll soon develop speed and confidence, and two-color knitting will be lots of fun and not a chore.

GAUGE

Many knitters face gauge with forboding. But it's really neither a mystery nor a hard concept to learn and love. I liken it to reading a map before taking an unknown trip. A gauge swatch helps you make sure everything is alright before you dive in. It can save you time ripping out mistakes and help you knit fearlessly, knowing that you have prepared for the project. I can't imagine embarking on a project without making a swatch. I just don't have enough time in my life to fool around with items that don't come out the right size.

Working a gauge swatch is simple: You knit a small piece of fabric with your chosen needles, yarn, and stitch pattern. After you've knit the pattern for about 4 inches (10 cm), bind off. Block the swatch by steaming it or washing it, and let it dry (see Washing and Blocking on page 204). Don't be tempted to skip blocking — it's a very important step! Blocking eliminates any unevenness in the fabric, so that you can lay it out neat and flat for measuring. In addition, water changes fiber, and since you'll want to wash most knitwear at some point, it's best to know how a yarn and stitch pattern react before you work up an entire project, rather than afterward.

Next, lay your swatch on a smooth, flat surface, and place a ruler across the stitches along a row. Count how many stitches there are in a 4-inch section of the fabric. Divide the number of stitches by 4 to get your "stitches per inch." Refer to your pattern to see if you're getting the number of stitches required. If you are, you're all set to start knitting. But what if it's not exactly right?

▶ **If you have more stitches** in the 4-inch (10 cm) section than you should, you are knitting too tightly (your stitches are too small). Change to a larger size needle and try again.

▶ **If you have fewer stitches** in the 4-inch (10 cm) section than you should, you are knitting too loosely

Measure up. Block your swatch, then lay it flat on a smooth surface. Count the number of stitches per inch to determine your gauge on the finished item.

(your stitches are too large). Change to a smaller size needle and try again.

A number of things can affect gauge. Some stitch patterns, such as ribs, cables, and Fair Isle, are tighter than plain Stockinette fabric, so you'll get more stitches per inch. Garter Stitch gauges are usually looser, since this stitch pattern tends to spread horizontally.

Other circumstances also affect gauge, some of which you can control, and others which you cannot. A gauge swatch gives you the number of stitches per inch that you are getting with your hands, needles, and yarn on a specific day, but your mood on a particular day may cause your knitting to be tight.

BALL BAND ADVICE

Gauge is usually given on the manufacturer's ball band. Use this as a guide, however, not a rule. Chances are your gauge will be different from the gauge given on the yarn label. Yarn companies provide a gauge to give you an idea of what to expect and what size needle to try first.

Sometimes the gauge of the same yarn differs from color to color. A gauge on the same yarn is often different depending on whether it is knit in the round or back and forth in rows. The list goes on and on. Trust me: To save time and anguish, check your own gauge on each yarn you knit with!

I designed the project Boot Toppers as a way to knit a gauge swatch and at the same time create something you can use. (See pages 68–71.)

surface decoration on knits

This is where the real fun starts. When you knit circularly in the traditional fashion using one or more colors, your project probably looks nice but still plain — "normal." If you add either duplicate stitch or embroidery stitches or both, however, you can transform your work into another decorated dimension. You can be as creative as you like, follow my directions or make up your own design. Most importantly, have fun with these new techniques.

DUPLICATE STITCH

Duplicate stitch is an easy technique I use to add a third, fourth, fifth, or sixth color to my Fair Isle two-color knitting. I'm a lazy knitter: I do what's easy for me, which means knitting only two-color Fair Isle. Then, to make the knitting prettier, more colorful, and more interesting, I add more colors in duplicate stitch. Magically, the finished fabric looks as if it had been knit in many colors. Only you'll know the truth that you added the extra colors when you were done with the knitting.

You'll need extra colors of yarn in the same weight as the knitting yarn and a blunt-tipped tapestry needle. (*Note:* It is very important not to use a sharp needle, as it will split the knitting yarn.)

With each pattern in this book that requires duplicate stitch, you'll find an extra chart showing where to add the duplicate stitch. Usually, the added stitches follow the outline of the pattern (such as a circle or diamond). After the first few duplicate stitches, in most cases you'll find you don't need to follow the chart.

1 Thread your blunt-tipped needle with the color yarn shown on the chart. Begin on the wrong side of the fabric directly under your first stitch. To anchor the working yarn, take two small stitches into one of the plies of the knitted stitch leaving a ¾" (2 cm) tail. These stitches shouldn't show on the right side. Come up through the bottom of the stitch you are covering.

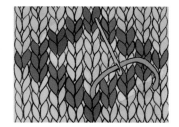

2 With tip of your needle, trace the knitted stitch by going under the two legs above the stitch you are covering. Pull the yarn through.

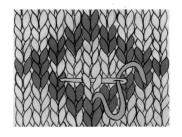

3 Take the yarn down where you came up (in the middle of the stitch). Don't pull the stitch too tight or the added color will be lost in the surface of the fabric.

4 Move on to the remaining stitch, keeping the yarn loose behind the work.

WORKING FAIR ISLE AND DUPLICATE STITCH CHARTS

Throughout the book, wherever I've designed duplicate stitch to be done over a Fair Isle design, you will find two charts: one for knitting and the other for embroidery. Follow the Fair Isle chart for the two-color knitting first, then when the item is completed, follow the second chart for placement of the duplicate stitches. The photo detail below shows the result of following the knit and embroider charts for the diamonds and stripes on the Persian Carpet Socks shown on page 96.

KNITTING

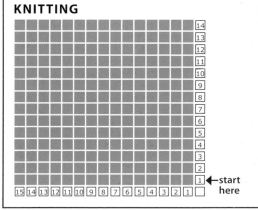

EMBROIDERY

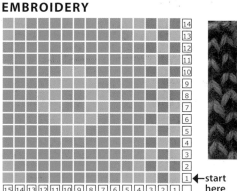

▸ **Loosen up.** Keep your stitching relaxed and loose; don't pull it tightly.

▸ **Ending off.** Always work on the right side of the fabric, slipping your needle across the backside and coming up where you need your next shot of color. The only time I turn my work over is when I am ending off a thread. To end off, just weave the tapestry needle through the backside of the fabric, preferably through the duplicate stitches.

▸ **Correcting mistakes.** If you make a mistake, un-thread the needle, then use it to unpick the stitch.

▸ **Which way to go.** Work the stitches diagonally or horizontally. If you fill vertical lines with duplicate stitches, they sometimes disappear. Right-handed knitters usually find it easiest to work from right to left, and left-handers from left to right.

▸ **Other uses.** You can add one, two, three, or more colors in duplicate stitch. When I find a mistake in my Fair Isle patterning, I use duplicate stitch to cover up the mistake with the correct color yarn.

EMBROIDERY STITCHES

To add more color and give my knitwear a third dimension, I use traditional embroidery stitches as decorative embellishment. The embroidered stitches sit on top of the fabric, sometimes following the Fair Isle pattern and sometimes decorating a solid-color area. Although adding embroidery to knitted fabric may look difficult and complex, it really is so easy. Just as with Fair Isle and duplicate stitch, the most important thing is to stitch loosely but neatly so that the fabric isn't distorted by the added stitches. You can learn hundreds of embroidery stitches, but I've used only a few on the projects in this book. I suggest you practice these stitches on a knitted swatch.

To begin, thread a blunt needle with your yarn, then, to anchor your yarn, take two stitches through one of the plies on the wrong side of the fabric, directly under your starting point; leave a ¾" (2 cm) tail. Come up through to the right side of the fabric.

To end, take two or three stitches through one of the plies on the wrong side, *or* weave the yarn through the backside of the embroidery stitches.

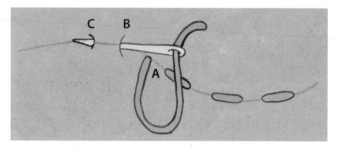

Running Stitch

The most basic stitch, Running Stitch, is quick and easy. Begin by drawing a line. Come up at A, and insert your needle at B. Come up at C, and pull the needle through. Continue along the line, keeping the stitches evenly spaced. Once you feel comfortable, you can take several stitches at once. You can work running stitch in free-form organic shapes or follow a row of stitches to decorate the fabric horizontally.

French Knot

French knots look like miniature bobbles added to the fabric. The knot often slips through to the wrong side of the fabric and disappears, so they can be a little tricky to master. Don't be discouraged: just be patient and try again. French knots are useful for outlining a

Fair Isle pattern (see page 175) or use them randomly for spotted decoration.

1 Come up through the knitted fabric preferably in the middle of a stitch. With your left hand (right hand, for lefties), wrap the thread twice around the needle.

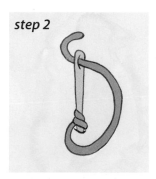

2 Rotate the needle toward the fabric, and insert the needle close to, but not into, the place where you came up. You can split a yarn or go down in the middle of a neighboring stitch. Pull tightly on the wraps as you do this, then draw the needle to the back, forming a knot on the surface. *Tip:* Go down about half a stitch to a full stitch away from where you came up, or the knot will disappear to the wrong side.

Chain Stitch

Chain Stitch looks like a series of attached loops. It can be used to create organic, loopy lines for vines and leaves, or it can follow a geometric pattern. You can also work it across a straight row of stitches to add a third dimension. To avoid distorting the fabric, take care not to pull the yarn too tightly. It doesn't matter whether you enter the fabric between stitches or pierce the yarn: do whatever you prefer. Always work from the right side of the fabric.

1 Come up at A. Take a stitch from B to C, but do not pull the needle through. Wrap the thread under the needle at C. Pull the needle through and

a loop will form on the top of the fabric. Continue by inserting your needle at D (inside the loop), then come up at E, again wrapping the yarn under the needle before you pull the needle through.

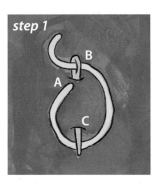
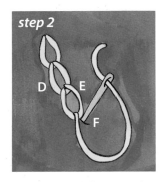

2 To end, insert your needle at F just outside the loop and pull to the back side to anchor the stitch.

Chain stitch vine on Floral and Tasseled Scarf shown on page 26.

Lazy Daisy

The Lazy Daisy Stitch is a variation of Chain Stitch, in which each "chain" is worked separately. The traditional daisylike flower is made by working individual chain stitches around a center point. Single lazy daisies can be used for leaves along a stem.

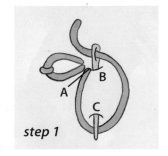

1 Come up at A. Insert your needle at B, and come

up at C, but do not pull the needle through. Wrap thread under needle at C, then pull needle through to form a loop. To avoid distorting the fabric, take care not to pull too tightly.

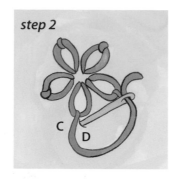
step 2

2 End the stitch by inserting the needle at D to anchor the loop. Work additional stitches, keeping the start of each stitch close to the center and working the "petals" so that they radiate out.

Spider Web

I love this stitch on knitwear! It makes a sculptural addition to the fabric.

1 *Base.* Come up where you want your spider web to be centered (A), and make a stitch from A to B. Make a series of radiating stitches from the center to form a circle (like spokes, from A to C, from A to D, and so on). Your base must have an odd number of stitches (5, 7, or 9, for instance), so that you can weave the "web."

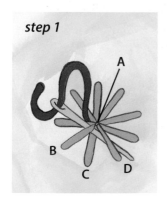
step 1

step 2

2 *Web.* Using the same or a different-color yarn threaded in a blunt-tip needle, come up again at the center. Weave over and under every other spoke, spiraling outward until the entire shape is filled. Pack the stitches down with the eye end of the needle to create a filled-in, sculptural weaving. End by drawing the yarn through to the back side under a spoke.

Bobbles

I love lumpy, bumpy bobbles! They add an interesting texture when used in traditional cable patterns, but knitted separately in a myriad of different colors, they can bring a truly playful feeling to your knitwear. I use the cast-on and cast-off tails to attach them to the knitted fabric as sculptural, colorful additions to many of my projects. Here's how to knit up a single bobble:

Set Up Cast on 1 stitch.
Row 1 (right side) Knit into the front, back, front, and back of the same stitch to make 4 stitches from the single cast-on stitch.
Rows 2 and 4 (wrong side) P4.
Row 3 K4.
Row 5 K4, pass second, third, and fourth stitches on needle over the first stitch to decrease back to 1 stitch.
Cut yarn, leaving a 5" (12.5 cm) tail, and fasten off last stitch.

Bobble sewn onto knitted fabric after it was completed.

other embellishments

Pompoms and tassels add a final fanciful, joyous touch to a project. Pompoms are downright bouncy, fun, and playful; tassels add a certain polish to a project. Both contribute color and zip to a plain piece of knitwear, transforming it into something out of the ordinary.

POMPOMS

Pompoms bring a fresh, festive touch to any knitwear they embellish. They make me think of being warmly wrapped in cozy woolens for an afternoon of ice skating or sledding.

You can purchase plastic pompom makers to help you make pompoms quickly, or you can easily make pompoms the old-fashioned way. Here's how:

1 Cut two pieces of cardboard, each 3" × 4" (7.5 × 10 cm). Hold the pieces of cardboard back to back, and wrap cellophane packing tape around them, covering all the edges with tape as you fasten the pieces together. (The tape makes it easy to slide the yarn off in step 3.)

2 Cut a piece of yarn about 10" (25 cm) long. Set this piece aside. (Plied yarn is best for this purpose, as it's stronger than single-ply yarn.)

3 Tightly wrap the pompom yarn around the cardboard, layering it as shown. The more yarn you wrap, the thicker and denser the pompom will be: 120 wraps makes a nice thick pompom. Cut the end of the yarn and carefully slide the bundle of yarn off the cardboard, keeping the bundle aligned and intact.

step 3

4 Wrap the 10" (25 cm) piece of yarn as tightly as you can around the bundle of yarn at the midpoint (like a cinched in waistline), and tie a firm

step 4

knot. Flip the pompom over and tie a second knot. Leave the ends of the tying yarn long. (You will use them to attach the pompom to your knitwear.) Cut the loops and trim any uneven strands to shape it to the size you desire.

SPICED-UP POMPOMS

> ▸ To make a multi-colored pompom, wind different colors of yarn in random amounts around the cardboard.
>
> ▸ To make a tweedy pompom, wrap two colors of yarn at the same time.

TASSELS

Adding tassels to hats, zipper pulls, and mitten cuffs gives an entirely new and folkloric feeling to humdrum pieces of clothing. Tassels remind me of celebrations — tassels decorate graduation caps everywhere each June. Andean herders place tassels on their llamas' ears to increase the animals' fertility.

You can make tassels any size you want, simply by changing the size of the cardboard you wrap the yarn around and/or varying the number of wraps. The instructions here are for a 4" (10 cm) tassel.

1 Cut two pieces of cardboard, each 3" × 4" (7.5 × 10 cm). Hold the pieces of cardboard back to back, and wrap cellophane packing tape around them, covering all the edges with tape as you fasten the pieces together. (The tape makes it easy to slide the yarn off in step 3.)

2 Cut two pieces of yarn about 10" (25 cm) long. (Use the same yarn you are using for the tassels or a stronger yarn, if the tassel yarn is loosely twisted.) Set these pieces aside.

3 Tightly wrap the tassel yarn around the cardboard, layering it as shown. The more yarn you wrap, the thicker and denser the tassel will be: 60 wraps makes a nice thick tassel. *Tip:* Wind two lengths of yarn at once to make your job quicker.

4 Thread one 10" (25 cm) length of yarn under the bundle of yarn at one end of the cardboard, and tie a double knot, leaving the ends long for attaching the tassel to the project. With sharp scissors, cut through the loops at the free (untied) end of the bundle. Slide the yarn off the cardboard.

5 Wrap the second 10" (25 cm) piece of yarn snugly around the bundle about 1" (2.5 cm) below the tie, and tie a knot. Flip the tassel over and tie a second knot. Thread these ends through a tapestry needle, and draw both ends to the inside of the tassel. Trim the tassel ends to neaten.

TASSEL TIP

You can make tweedy looking tassels by winding several colors of yarn together at the same time.

6 Use the loose ends at the top of the tassel to attach it by threading each end through a needle separately and using the needle to draw the end to the wrong side of the item you are embellishing. Tie the two ends on the wrong side to secure.

more knitting techniques

Learning to knit is a gradual evolution. There are so many knitting techniques to explore that it's virtually impossible to know them all. Here are a few fun ones to add to your repetoire and increase your skills. You'll need them for some of the projects in this book.

BACKWARD LOOP CAST ON

I use this easy increase method frequently. Abbreviation M1 (Make 1) used throughout this book refers to this method. Form a loop with the yarn and place it on the right needle. Pull it tight. On the next row, work it as you do any other stitch. The increase will disappear into the work.

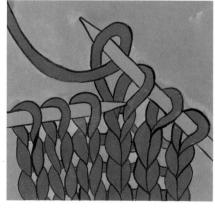

Backward loop increase.

Mitered corner of Floral and Tasseled Scarf shown on page 26.

MITERED CORNERS

I like to miter square corners on my knitwear. You can see examples of mitered corners on the red scarf (page 27) and the embroidered cardigan (page 175). It is very easy to do and a fun way to make a plain object look fancy. Once you learn the technique, you'll find all kinds of uses for it, including at necklines, along bottom edges, or all the way around a scarf or afghan. You'll need circular needles and stitch markers.

Set Up Using a circular needle, pick up the edge stitches all the way around the knitted object. To mark the beginning of each mitered corner, place a marker on each side of each corner stitch.

Round 1 Increase one stitch before the marker, slip the marker, work the corner stitch as desired (I like to keep my corner stitches in Stockinette Stitch), slip the second marker, then increase 1 stitch after corner stitch: You have increased 2 stitches at the mitered corner. For the increase, I use a simple increase made by placing a backward loop on the needle.

Round 2 Work all the stitches without any increases.

Round 3 Work two increases at each corner as in Round 1.

DOUBLE-POINTED NEEDLES

Perhaps you've always been fascinated seeing a knitter work on double-pointed needles, but you've been too chicken to try it. Now you want to knit socks, so this is it, your time to unravel the mystery of double-pointed needles! (You *can* knit socks "back and forth," but having a seam up one side of a sock is just darn uncomfortable.) Next thing you know, you'll be making hats, mittens, and more, all knit in the round.

1 Use two needles to cast on the required number of stitches. Add a third needle, and divide the stitches so that there are about the same number of stitches on each of the three needles.

2 Form the needles into a triangle, manipulate the stitches so the cast-on edge stitches all lie in the same direction, and begin knitting with the fourth needle. It's important to keep those stitches all facing the same direction and not twisted around the needle. You want your knitting to grow off the needles into a perfect tube. If the knitting is twisted, you have no choice but to pull your work out and begin again.

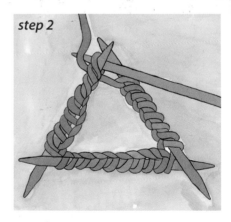

step 2

When you reach the end of the first needle, use the now-empty needle to go ahead and knit stitches on the second needle. Continue all the way around. To avoid loose stitches developing at the point where you move from one needle to the next, knit the first two stitches of each needle extra tight.

The fun thing about double-pointed needles is you are never sure where the round began. Knitting with double-pointed needles becomes one of those knitting mind games: Try to stop after one more row. You can't! You just keep furiously knitting away as your tube grows and grows, and pretty soon, you've got a sock or mittens or even a sweater.

It's possible to use more than four double-pointed needles at once if you're knitting a very large piece. Usually you turn to circular needles for these kinds of projects, but when you don't have the right size circular, in a pinch you can use 5 or 6 or more double-pointed needles.

Carrying double-pointed needles is tricky because they can slide out of the work. Use stitch protectors or rubber bands to keep the stitches from slipping off the needles.

TURNING A HEEL

Turning a heel is done to alter a knitted tube so that it fits around the heel of a foot. It is done by making a series of *short rows* (rows that are not knit completely across) after you knit the sock's *heel flap*. As you follow the directions for the heel given for each sock pattern, you'll see the shaping build up as you work these short rows. It isn't hard to do and, after the first few rows, you'll catch on.

GRAFTING

This technique is used to join the last stitches on the toes of socks without making a bumpy seam. Divide your remaining stitches between two needles. Hold the two needles together so that the stitches align, with wrong sides of the sock facing. (**Note** To make the drawings clearer, the needles are not shown. However, when you are grafting, do *not* remove stitches from needles until indicated by instructions in steps 3 and 4.)

1 Thread the yarn tail through a blunt-tip needle. Insert the needle through the first stitch of the front as shown. Draw the yarn through, but leave the stitch on the needle.

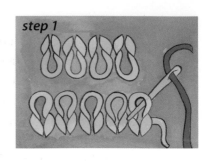
step 1

2 Insert the needle through the first stitch on the back needle as shown. Draw the yarn through, but leave the stitch on the needle.

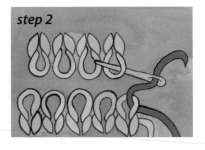
step 2

3 Insert the needle through the first stitch on the front needle as shown. Slip the stitch off the needle. Insert the needle through the second stitch on the front needle as shown. Leave stitch on needle. Tighten the yarn.

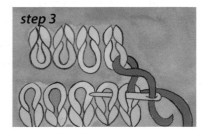
step 3

4 Insert the needle through the first stitch on the back needle as shown. Slip stitch off needle. Insert needle through second stitch of back needle as shown. Leave stitch on needle. Tighten yarn. Repeat steps 3 and 4 until no stitches remain on needles. Weave in tail end of yarn to tighten and neaten.

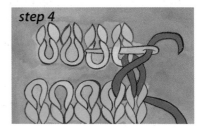
step 4

STEEKING

I am here to calm all your fears about the dreaded steek. I've never been afraid of steeks and have always assumed this was because I'm comfortable using a sewing machine. But, if you're less familiar with machine stitching, I'm here to say, "Be unafraid!" In all the years that I have worked steeks and worn steeked sweaters, I have never had one fall apart or unravel. This is a tried-and-true, time-tested technique.

A *steek* is a narrow section of Stockinette Stitches developed to provide a place to cut along to create openings in circularly knit garments. Before the opening is cut, the steek stitches are reinforced by a line of stitching (I prefer machine stitching for this purpose). Commonly, you'll find steeks at the openings of cardigans, sleeves, and necklines. The advantage of knitting a steek is that you can work in the round with the right side of the fabric facing you, which makes it easier to follow a Fair Isle chart (see page 195). The steek stitches are usually knit using both the colors in the pattern. This catches them into the fabric, making the steek stronger and keeping both colors neat and taut when cut.

Although steeks are traditionally and ideally used when knitting Fair Isle, I also make steeks in almost all the solid-color sweaters I knit. And I like to use them in places many people wouldn't think of. For instance, the Navajo-Inspired Afghan (page 34) uses a steek so that it can be worked in the round, and the Coleus Scarf (page 30) uses a steek for the same reason.

As with all new techniques, it's best to practice on a swatch. You can make all the mistakes you want and throw the piece out when you're finished. You can work a practice steek on any swatch you have lying around. It needn't be Fair Isle. The point of making a swatch steek is to get you feeling more comfortable cutting handknit fabric before you cut into your first completed garment.

1 Using a sewing machine set on a medium-size zigzag stitch, stitch down the two center stitches of the steek section as shown in the illustration. Now using a sewing machine set on a normal-length straight stitch, sew a straight line in the ditch between the last stitch of the pattern and the first stitch of the steek. Do this on both sides of the steek.

2 Now, pull yourself together, swallow hard, and find some sharp scissors. Cut between the two center rows of zigzag stitching to separate the piece into two sections. That's all there is to it. Not hard at all — you'll wonder what all the fuss was about.

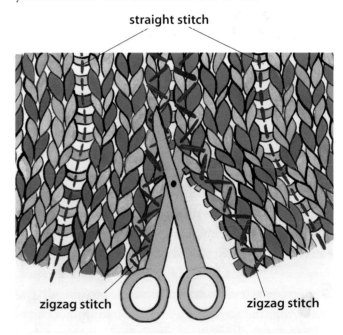

Working straight and zigzag stitches to secure steek, before cutting between the zigzag stitches.

finishing techniques

WASHING AND BLOCKING

As far as I am concerned, a knitted garment isn't finished until it has been washed and blocked.